THE ARTFUL STORYBOOK

THE ARTFUL STORYBOOK
Mixed-Media Artists Create Handmade Tales

terry taylor

LARK BOOKS

A Division of Sterling Publishing Co., Inc.
New York / London

Library of Congress Cataloging-in-Publication Data

The artful storybook : mixed media artists create handmade tales. — 1st ed.
    p. cm.
  Includes index.
  ISBN-13: 978-1-60059-143-3 (pb-trade pbk. : alk. paper)
  ISBN-10: 1-60059-143-4 (pb-trade pbk. : alk. paper)
  1. Handicraft. 2. Scrapbook journaling. 3. Short story—Authorship.
TT157.A7725 2008
  745.593—dc22

                        2007037091

10 9 8 7 6 5 4 3 2 1

First Edition

Published by Lark Books, A Division of
Sterling Publishing Co., Inc.
387 Park Avenue South, New York, NY 10016

Text © 2008, Lark Books
Photography © 2008, Lark Books unless otherwise specified

Distributed in Canada by Sterling Publishing,
c/o Canadian Manda Group, 165 Dufferin Street
Toronto, Ontario, Canada M6K 3H6

Distributed in the United Kingdom by GMC Distribution Services,
Castle Place, 166 High Street, Lewes, East Sussex, England BN7 1XU

Distributed in Australia by Capricorn Link (Australia) Pty Ltd.,
P.O. Box 704, Windsor, NSW 2756 Australia

If you have questions or comments about this book, please contact:
Lark Books
67 Broadway
Asheville, NC 28801
828-253-0467

Manufactured in China

ISBN 13: 978-1-60059-143-3
ISBN 10: 1-60059-143-4

For information about custom editions, special sales, premium and corporate purchases, please
contact Sterling Special Sales Department at 800-805-5489 or specialsales@sterlingpub.com.

EDITOR:
Linda Kopp

EDITORIAL ASSISTANCE:
Amanda Carestio,
Kathleen McCafferty

ART DIRECTION:
828, Inc.

COVER DESIGNER:
Cindy LaBreacht

PHOTOGRAPHER:
Stewart O'Shields

CONTENTS

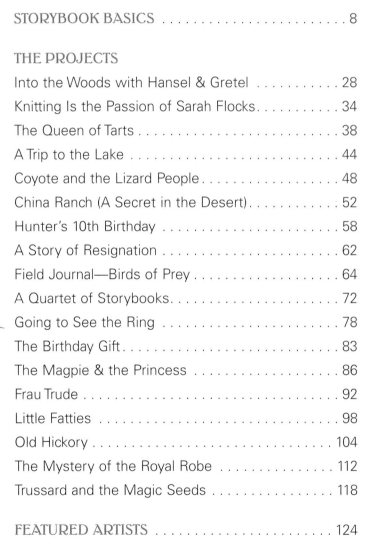

INTRODUCTION

ONCE UPON A TIME . . .

I've always loved storybooks. This author portrait—as a snappily dressed 4 year old—was staged by the photographer. That book wasn't mine! My Mother Goose—*Mom saved all of my childhood books—is pictured on page 14. It was a present from my kindergarten teacher for graduation. My nephews have almost all of my books now, but I've held on to a few special titles to reread. I still love a good storybook.*

~ Terry Taylor

Even if those particular words don't begin every storybook tale, the sense of wonder and magic they invoke are part and parcel of our childhood experiences with storybooks. Many adults—myself among them—have never outgrown the thrill of discovery that waits for us inside a storybook. It's no surprise that many of us vividly remember the specific style of the illustrations, the thread of the storylines, and even the size and format of our favorite storybooks.

As a "grown up," I'll bet you've lovingly crafted handmade cards for special occasions, created memory albums or scrapbooks, and perhaps even explored altered books. In all of those forms you've worked with imagery and words, and that's why the storybook format is such a wonderful canvas to add to your creative repertoire.

In storybooks you can reinterpret well-known, traditional tales of princesses, ogres, and knights as well as write and illustrate original stories about your beloved cat (or dog), exotic journeys, or simple camping trips. If you think about it, the stories in many

classic storybooks deal with "adult" themes—loss of parents, the battle between good and evil, the search for love, and triumph over adversity. Storybooks appeal to that part within us that longs to hear a story—funny, scary, salacious, tragic, or melancholy—coupled with visuals that enrich the written words.

Storybooks can be illustrated using a variety of techniques—rubber stamping, collage, simple drawing, stitchery, and more. Illustrate the story you've chosen to tell using skills and techniques that you're comfortable with, even if that medium isn't used in the pages that follow. I can think of many other art and craft techniques that would make wonderful storybook illustrations.

In *The Artful Storybook* I've invited a variety of artists who eagerly agreed to explore the storybook form. Each artist approached it in his or her own unique way. Jane Reeves and Karen Shelton retold the classic story of *The Princess and the Pea* using distinctly different styles. Andrea Stern created a multi-layered, stitched, and embroidered page from one of Hans Christian Andersen's lesser-known stories. Terry Garrett revisited the tale of *Hansel and Gretel*, encasing his accordion-fold book in a wooden house.

The painter Julie Armbruster crafted her storybook based on the paintings she creates. On page 104, graphic artist Susan McBride collaborated with book artist Annie Fain Liden to create her richly illustrated story of one childhood summer. Erikia Ghumm's story about her dog's tenth birthday is lovingly illustrated with personal photographs. Linda and Opie O'Brien's *The Mystery of the Royal Robe*—bones and all—is a tour de force of mixed-media art. And Margert Kruljac drew her inspiration for a set of books based on stories her children and their friends dictated to her.

Each of the artists has something to tell us about their creative processes or childhood experiences with storybooks. In most cases, I've tried to show you the complete book each artist created. It was easy to show you the entire story contained in a matchbook but not so easy to choose representative pages from Amy Blandford's densely illustrated and text-filled book (page 64).

Go ahead and rush to the lushly illustrated pages in this book. I know you can't wait to start the story. Have an inspired peek, then start your own storybook, and…

LIVE HAPPILY EVER AFTER.

STORYBOOK BASICS

I was raised by a reader in a family of readers. Every week we would make a trip to the library, where I would get the four books allowed on my children's card, and my mother would check several others out for me. I'd disappear into the worlds where these stories would take me, sometimes to the point of not hearing anything in my surroundings, even my name, until someone physically touched my arm. As the oldest of four children, the escape into storybooks was a joyous necessity!

~ LK Ludwig

A Brief History

LONG, LONG AGO, stories were passed orally from person to person. Prior to the invention of the printed book, stories that were written down were read, or read aloud, by the educated few. Even with Gutenberg's invention of movable type around 1450, books created especially for children were rarely produced for another 300 years. Children were thought of as miniature adults, and certain subjects in books printed for adults—religious or moral education, grammar, mathematics, and etiquette—were deemed suitable for their education. The few illustrations that were printed in these books were small black-and-white woodcuts or engravings.

John Newbery (1713–1767) is generally considered to be one of the first publishers of books created especially for children. *A Little Pretty Pocket-Book* appeared in 1744, and the most popular of his books, *The History of Little Goody Two Shoes*, was published in 1766. Read how little Margery Meanwell became a "trotting tutor" teaching neigh-

borhood children to read or her "lessons for the conduct of life," and you'll never again wonder about the origins of that epithet.

In the nineteenth century, the concept of "childhood" as a distinct period of life fostered a different way of thinking about children. At the same time, printing technologies grew by leaps

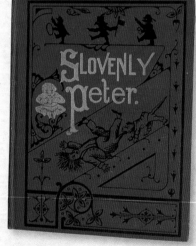

Slovenly Peter or Cheerful Stories and Funny Pictures (Struwwelpeter)
Heinrich Hoffman
John C. Wintson Company
Philadelphia, ca. 1925
Collection of The Captain's Bookshelf, Asheville, N.C

and bounds during the industrial revolution. Illustrated books—first in black and white, then lavish color—were created for both adults and children in large numbers.

Heinrich Hoffman's *Der Struwwelpeter*— Shockhead Peter or Slovenly Peter—was a bestseller in 1845. Originally written and illustrated for Hoffman's

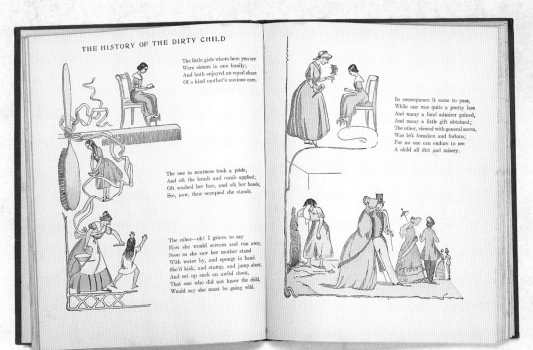

son, Heinrich was persuaded by friends and patients to publish the tale. From a modern point of view, the stories seem macabre. They were meant to scare children when they behaved badly and broke the rules of their parents. Thumbs are cut away with big scissors for sucking one's thumbs, minor faults are punished by death, and, in the story of *Little Pauline*, a girl who plays with matches burns into ashes.

One of the first celebrity book illustrators of this period was Randolph Caldecott (1846–1886). It's estimated that 867,000 copies of his popular illustrated books were sold. Titles such as *The House that Jack Built*, *Sing a Song of Sixpence*, *Hey Diddle Diddle*, and *Baby Bunting* were read and treasured by many Victorian children.

Storybooks of the twentieth century are the ones we're most familiar with, even if some are based on earlier stories. These storybooks married text and illustration as never before. Authors such as Seuss, Sendak, Van Allsburg, L'Engle, Cleary, Lobel, and Bemelmans are household names. We can picture in our mind's eye the vivid and unique illustrations of Greenway, Rackham, Seuss, Sendak, Tudor, Carle, and others. Both the creative stories and vivid illustrations of these luminaries have shaped our perception and definition of storybooks.

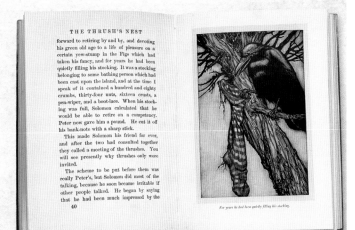

AWARD WINNING STORYBOOKS

Here are some titles that have won either the Newbery or Caldecott Medal. Each year the American Library Association (ALA) awards these two highly coveted medals for outstanding children's literature published in the previous year.

The tradition began in 1922 with the creation of the Newbery Medal, the first ever children's book award. It's named in honor of the 18th-century bookseller, John Newbery.

In 1937 the Caldecott Medal was established for illustrators of children's literature. The ALA recognized that artists were just as important as the authors and equally deserving of praise. The medal is given in honor of English illustrator Randolph Caldecott who produced dynamically illustrated books for children.

Here are some award-winning titles you'll fondly remember, some you'll no doubt want to reread, and others you may want to discover for the first time. Also included in the list are Honor Books—runner-up titles recognized each year for outstanding quality by the ALA. For a complete list of medal winners, visit these ALA websites: www.ala.org/alsc/caldecott.html or www.ala.org/alsc/newbery.html.

Take a look—is one of your favorites on the list?

Newbery Medal Winners
1923 *The Voyages of Doctor Dolittle* by Hugh Lofting
1936 *Caddie Woodlawn* by Carol Ryrie Brink
1949 *King of the Wind* by Marguerite Henry
1961 *Island of the Blue Dolphins* by Scott O'Dell
1963 *A Wrinkle in Time* by Madeleine L'Engle
1970 *Sounder* by William H. Armstrong

1972 *Mrs. Frisby and the Rats of NIMH* by Robert C. O'Brien
1978 *Bridge to Terabithia* by Katherine Paterson
1982 *A Visit to William Blake's Inn: Poems for Innocent and Experienced Travelers* by Nancy Willard

Honor Books
Ramona Quimby, Age 8 by Beverly Cleary
My Brother Sam is Dead by James Lincoln Collier & Christopher Collier
Frog and Toad Together by Arnold Lobel
Rascal: A Memoir of a Better Era by Sterling North
Old Yeller by Fred Gipson
Charlotte's Web by E. B. White
Misty of Chincoteague by Marguerite Henry
Little Town on the Prairie by Laura Ingalls Wilder
Mr. Popper's Penguins by Richard & Florence Atwater

Caldecott Medal Winners
1942 *Make Way for Ducklings* by Robert McCloskey
1954 *Madeline's Rescue* by Ludwig Bemelmans
1964 *Where the Wild Things Are* by Maurice Sendak
1970 *Sylvester and the Magic Pebble* by William Steig
1982 *Jumanji* by Chris Van Allsburg
1986 *The Polar Express* by Chris Van Allsburg

Honor Books
Madeline by Ludwig Bemelmans
Mother Goose, illustrated by Tasha Tudor
McElligot's Pool by Dr. Seuss
Goggles! by Ezra Jack Keats
Frog and Toad are Friends by Arnold Lobel
Anansi the Spider: A Tale from the Ashanti, adapted and illustrated by Gerald McDermott
The Stinky Cheese Man and Other Fairly Stupid Tales, illustrated by Lane Smith, text by Jon Scieszka

The fairy tales of the Brothers Grimm have always fascinated me, actually more now as an adult than when I was a small child. I find many of them to be pretty high up there on the "creepy scale"—rather dark and with a moralistic twist. Just right for an artist's interpretation!

~ Terry Garrett

What's Your Story?

IF YOU'RE THINKING that you can't possibly begin to create an original story for a storybook, you're wrong. Stop and think: you're already a story-teller. You tell stories every day—over the dinner table at home, at family reunions, on hastily scribbled vacation postcards, standing around the water cooler, or explaining why your "homework" is late. Any of those stories could become the basis of a storybook.

If you're still not convinced you could write a story, but have the urge to create a storybook, then put your own spin on a classic tale. That's a simple and direct way to start. You know by heart many stories from your childhood. Perhaps it's one of Aesop's fables, a bowd-lerized version of a Brothers Grimm tale, or even a story drawn from your spiritual upbringing. You have a whole library of stories to draw from. Dust off those old favorites you memorized as a child, and use them as a starting point for your storybook creation.

Old Tales of Japan
Yuri Yasuda
Illustrations by Yoshinobu Sakakura and Eiichi Mitsui
Charles E. Tuttle Company
Tokyo 1960
Collection of the author

If favorite fairy tales and fables don't inspire you, use a historical event or personage as the basis of your story as Catherine Moore did in her storybook (page 38). Don't be shy about retelling myths from different countries and civilizations. And, by all means, feel free to use events or characters from real life (yours or someone else's) as a basis for a storybook. It's a good idea not to be libelous!

Once you have an idea for a storybook you'd like to create, whether it's an original story or your retelling of a familiar tale, I suggest that you simply put pen to paper or tap it out on your keyboard.

It's that simple. Remember the English teacher who instructed you to write a rough draft, ignoring spelling and grammatical errors? You should follow those directions when you begin to write your story.

A rough draft allows you to get the basic bones of the story—the dramatic structure—on paper. And don't let a phrase like "dramatic structure" frighten you. Even the stories you tell your coworkers may follow this five-point structure (see the sidebar on page 13). An even simpler way of thinking about story structure is this:

every story has a beginning, middle, and an ending.

However, we all know that not every story starts with the beginning. Novelists and movie directors structure the arc of their stories as they see fit. You should too. It's perfectly acceptable to begin a storybook with the climactic event from the end of a story, and then work your way back to the beginning to explain how it all happened. It's called artistic license.

Your rough draft gives you something tangible to look at. Even if you did print it, it's not perfect or set in stone. Now's your chance to add and subtract words, change the phrasing, rearrange the events, or transform a red riding hood into a pale blue anorak if it suits your purposes. Use a red pencil—just as Mrs. Jones did—if you wish.

Most writers set their work aside and come back later to revisit what they've written. I suggest you do the same. Once you're happy with what you've written, this text becomes the skeleton of the storybook you're about to create. Mrs. Jones would be so proud of you!

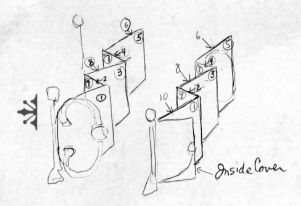

Before we begin any book project, we always start with a storyboard on a large sheet of newsprint. It makes it easier to track the progression of the story's words and imagery. The front and back of the pages are especially important. The placement of objects on a page and their methods of attachment need to be considered, so that if the attachments go through a page, they won't interfere with what's on the reverse side. The Mystery of the Royal Robe *demanded many boards, from the initial newsprint layout to several individual page templates.*

~ Linda & Opie O'Brien

What's the Plan?

ONCE YOU'VE CHOSEN THE STORY for your storybook, plan how you're going to attack the physical processes of making it. There's no single right way to go about it. One artist may start with rough page sketches or a spreadsheet with images, notes, and text mapped out. On the other hand, another artist may jump right in and create a cover before any pages are planned.

No matter what your working habits are, there are obvious questions you should consider before working on your storybook. Some of us do it intuitively; some of us need reminding to look before we leap.

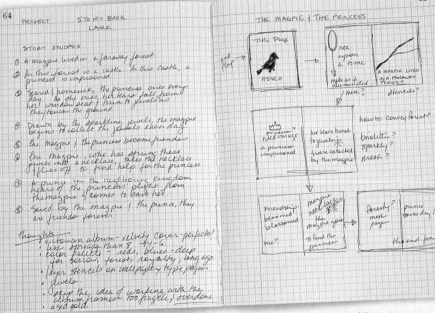

LK Ludwig

🌀 What format do you envision for your storybook? Is it a scroll, a simple stitched pamphlet, or an elaborately bound handmade book? Are you going to alter a child's board book or use a commercially bound blank book?

🌀 How are you going to illustrate your book? Are you using colored pencils, combining paint and collage, or even stitching? Are you longing to add three-dimensional embellishments? Your answer will dictate the type of page material you'll need for the storybook.

Terry Taylor

How are you going to present the words on the page? Is hand lettering appealing, or are you more of a rubber stamp junkie? Do you have a handheld label maker you're itching to use, or do you want to experiment with different fonts on the computer screen?

Once you've answered at least one of those questions, you may be tempted to get right to work on your storybook. But before you make the first cut, hole punch, or brush stroke, allow me to advise you to consider an additional aspect of your storybook. How do your design choices interact with each other? Each decision you make affects another aspect of the work.

When you've decided how to illustrate the story, how the text will appear on the page, and which format your storybook will take, then it's time to get to work. You can dive right in—if that's your style—or plan and experiment to your heart's delight.

Take a look at a preliminary study (page 15) for a storybook that Jane Reeves suggested creating for this book. Jane has brought together treatments for the cover, page style, illustrations, and text. It's a comprehensive illustration of the planning process.

DRAMATIC STRUCTURE

The format of a story from "once upon a time" to "happily ever after" follows what is known as dramatic structure. Within this structure are five points that keep the story moving along toward the finish: exposition, rising action, climax, falling action, and denouement or catastrophe, depending on whether the story is a comedy or tragedy.

Exposition occurs at the beginning of the story. Characters, setting, and the basic plot are introduced. Included at this point is also the inciting action, the event or introduction of conflict that acts as a catalyst for the rest of the story. In Cinderella's story, the exposition tells us that a beautiful young girl lives with her evil stepmother and ugly stepsisters. The inciting action is the revelation that, since her father's death, her stepfamily forces Cinderella to work as a servant.

The *rising action* follows, expanding on the main conflict and perhaps containing secondary conflicts that obstruct the main character from reaching his or her goal. In Cinderella, the rising action takes shape in her stepfamily's attempts to prevent Cinderella from going to the ball.

The *climax* is the turning point of the story. In many stories the main character ends up better off at the end than at the beginning; the reverse happens in a tragedy. The appearance of Cinderella's magical fairy godmother, who arrives to send Cinderella to the ball, is a climactic scene.

In the *falling action*, the conflict is resolved, with the main character winning or losing. However, there may also be a point of suspense in which the final outcome is questionable. The falling action in Cinderella takes place when she must flee the ball, losing her slipper; the suspense occurs when her stepmother tries to keep her from trying on the slipper.

The story's *conclusion* is found in the *denouement* or *catastrophe*, in which the final outcome of the story is revealed and loose ends are often tied up. In Cinderella, the main character lives "happily ever after," and the story's villains are punished.

Choosing a Book Format

THINK BACK to your favorite storybooks. What made them appealing to you? I liked the heft of my *Mother Goose* and the exotic (at least to my third-grade sense of style) slipcase presentation of my *Old Tales of Japan*.

A book (unless it's in a scroll form) has any number of pages and a cover. But *you* know it isn't quite that simple, is it? Books are made with different types of bindings, come in an assortment of shapes, and can be found in a wide variety of sizes. You can make your own storybook by folding and binding the pages, but what if you have no desire to do that? Consider using a book that's already made, it doesn't make your storybook any less artful. If it has pages and a cover, use it! A spiral-bound, lined notebook will work as will a blank sketchbook or an accountant's ledger. And don't forget books that are already printed. Picture the story of the gingerbread man re-created on the pages of a used cookbook or Rapunzel's tale presented in a vintage hair-styling manual. The possibilities are endless.

THE PRINCESS & THE PEA RE-IMAGINED

ARTIST
Jane Reeves

For her interpretation of the familiar Hans Christian Andersen tale, Jane envisioned altering a hardback book. Rather than altering the existing pages, Jane proposed that she remove them and use only the cover for her book. She created a mock-up of a hardbound book cover—front, back, and spine—then cut it into the castle shape she pictured in her mind.

Rather than creating pages to be bound into the cover, Jane proposed inserting an accordion fold format. She used a heavy cardstock to create a mock-up of the pages, piecing the cardstock together as needed to create a workable length.

Jane frequently uses collage elements in her work. She imagined scanning images, resizing them, and converting them to black and white, much like the images in her storybook on page 44. Decorative papers would serve as background for the collaged elements, which would be embellished with various media.

For the story text, Jane wanted to compose it on the computer in order to experiment with different fonts. She visualized aging the paper with ink, and perhaps tearing or cutting the edges of the printed text to give the pages visual interest.

Once upon a time there was a Handsome Prince who was very sad because he could not find a Real Princess to marry.

The King and Queen were distraught. "You must choose someone," they said.

One dark and stormy night a timid tap-tap was heard at the castle door. "Raise the portcullis," roared the King, and the maid ran to open the gate. Outside stood a beautiful girl who was very cold.

Altering Printed Books

Create a storybook by altering a printed book purchased from a secondhand source. Scout out the shelves in your local thrift shop for a treasure trove of choices. Be sure to choose a book that's sturdy and intact to work on. You can overlook dinged corners, but if the spine is falling apart, why take the time to rebind it properly?

Take a good look at the pages of a book before you purchase it. The pages in older books are often too yellowed, fragile, and brittle to work on. Be on the lookout for pages printed on heavy stock; they make a great "canvas." You may or may not choose to incorporate parts of the printed text and illustrations in your storybook.

You can embellish single pages in a book with simple collage, rubber-stamped images, or drawing with dry mediums such as a pencil or chalk. However, if you want to use fluid mediums, such as paints or inks, or you wish to add heavy elements to your pages, you'll need to strengthen them to prevent wrinkling or tearing.

Adding paper to single pages is also an excellent way to add color, hide printing, and strengthen them at the same time. Thin decorative papers—tissue papers, oriental papers, or dress patterns—work well. Cut two pieces of paper to your page size or slightly larger. Spread a thin layer of acrylic medium on a single page. Lay the decorative paper on the page and burnish it with a bone folder. Repeat this process on the back of the page. Otherwise, the page will warp and wrinkle. Use waxed paper to protect the page and press it flat overnight. Once the page is dry, you have a blank surface to work on.

If you're planning on attaching heavy elements to your storybook pages, consider gluing several pages together using a glue stick before you cover them with thin paper. And don't limit yourself to the size of pages in your book—cut them to any size you want, fold them, or remove them entirely.

And what about using the cover of a printed book? You can collage on the cover without much preparation. If you want to paint or draw on areas of the cover, prepare it with one or more coats of gesso. The gesso will obscure any illustration or lettering and prepare the surface for paints or other media. You might even consider taking apart a secondhand book and using the cover as a part of a handmade book.

Children's board books make great bases for artful storybooks, especially if you like to use paints and inks. Their thick and smooth pages are a delight to work on. Prepare board books by lightly sanding the pages to prepare the surface, then give each page one or more coats of white gesso. And if you want to make a uniquely shaped book, board books are easy to cut with a sharp craft knife or a small electric jigsaw. You can even find shaped board books—a car, a house, and other simple shapes—for your storybook.

Karen Shelton

Handmade Books

Bookmaking is a fine art. There are many ways to create handmade books—too many ways to give you a complete survey here. If you're enticed with thoughts of intricate Coptic bindings or tooled and gilded leather covers, you'll need to look—where else?—in other books. I've compiled a helpful list of books to consult if you want to make more complex handmade projects than simple pamphlets or accordion books.

The pages and covers of handmade books can be created with many different types of paper. Consider the type of book you're going to make before you choose the paper to make it with.

Will your book be constantly handled? If so you might want to use heavier papers such as watercolor paper or heavy cardstock.

What kind of media are you going to use when you illustrate your pages? A paper with a smooth finish—plate or hot press—is just right for ink; a paper with a bit more tooth—cold press—is a good choice for pastels or charcoal. Watercolors and acrylic paints are best used on rough finish papers.

How will the paper reflect the content of your book? Delicate rice paper might be appropriate for a Chinese fairy tale, papyrus for an Egyptian tale of pharaohs and pyramids. Lined pages, torn from notebooks, might be a nice base for a story about high school crushes.

BOOKS ON BOOKMAKING

Cover to Cover (1998)
Shereen LaPlantz

Bookworks: Books, Memory and Photo Albums, Journals and Diaries Made by Hand (1998)
Sue Doggett

Non-Adhesive Binding: Books without Paste or Glue (1999)
Keith A. Smith

The Essential Guide to Making Handmade Books (2000)
Gabrielle Fox

Making Books by Hand: A Step-by-Step Guide (2000)
Mary McCarthy

More Making Books by Hand: Exploring Miniature Books, Alternative Structures, and Found Objects (2004)
Peter Thomas

The Penland Book of Handmade Books: Master Classes in Bookmaking Techniques (2004)

Books Unbound (2005)
Michael Jacobs

The Decorated Journal (2006)
Gwen Diehn

Expressive Handmade Books (2006)
Alisa Golden

Fabric Memory Books (2007)
Lesley Riley

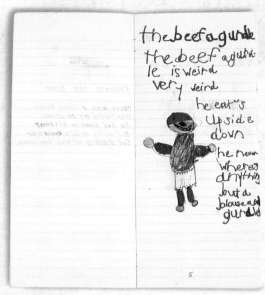

Karen Shelton

The Simple Pamphlet

In its simplest form, the pamphlet is an incredibly easy book to make. Stack four sheets of copy paper and fold them in half. Looks like a book, doesn't it? But the pages fall apart; they need to be held together. You could staple them along the folded edge, but that isn't very attractive and the pages won't lie flat. A more sophisticated and versatile version is the stitched pamphlet.

Once you've decided on a size for your pages and assembled them along with a slightly larger cover, you're ready to stitch the pages together. Open up your book and lay it flat with the cover facing up.

Use an awl or pushpin to prick three evenly spaced holes along the fold. Be sure you make your holes all the way through the stack.

Thread a needle with waxed linen or heavy thread. Begin sewing from the outside (or inside) center hole (figure 1). If you start on the outside, you'll end up back on the outside (and vice versa). Sew up and out through the top hole (figure 2), then down to the bottom hole (figure 3). Sew back up and out through the center hole (figure 4). Knot or tie a bow in your sewing thread (figure 5).

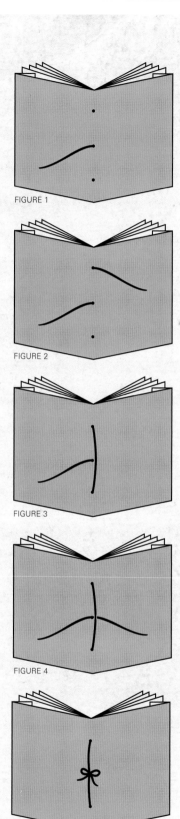

FIGURE 1

FIGURE 2

FIGURE 3

FIGURE 4

FIGURE 5

If your pamphlet is large or you want more stability in your pages, you can make a five-hole pamphlet. Start your stitching in the center and work your way up the top two holes in the spine, then back down, skipping the center hole.

Folded Books

There are many kinds of folded books. Some folded books (mazes) are created from single sheets with specially placed cuts. Others are created from single, folded sheets.

An accordion book, also known as concertina or leporello, is a simple form of folded book. A basic accordion-fold book, if the pages are made of stiff paper, won't need a cover. The pages can be square, rectangular, triangular, or even circular in shape with a bit of careful planning.

The concertina fold is best suited to rectangular or square shapes. First, determine the measurements for a single page. Next, calculate the length of paper you'll need by multiplying the width of a page by the number of pages you need. If you don't have paper long enough, you can create longer lengths by overlapping and gluing ends together.

You can carefully measure, mark, and fold each page one at a time, but an easier method is to fold the length of paper in half, then fold each half in half again with the edges folded toward the center. Figures 1 through 5 show you just how to proceed. Take care that the edges match as you fold.

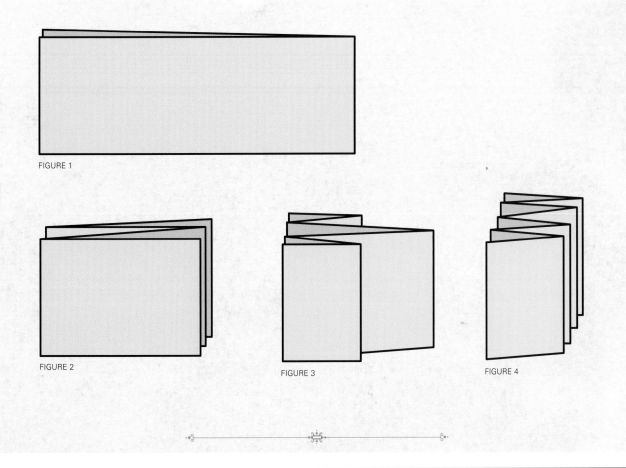

FIGURE 1

FIGURE 2

FIGURE 3

FIGURE 4

"I have a big lunch, Ooloo. You must help me eat it."

Sam took the food from his saddlebag and gave it all to the boy. He pretended he was still dizzy and couldn't eat.

Ooloo ate as if he were starved. "Hungry long time," he said.

"You'll not be hungry again," said Sam. "Who lets you go hungry anyway?"

"You keep secret?"

"Yes."

The Indian looked into Sam's honest blue eyes and was satisfied.

"Run away—hide in cave here—no food—two days no food."

"Who did you run away from? Your tribe?"

"No, No! My tribe Cherokee—far away— maybe thousand miles."

"How did you get here?"

Then he was pulled back—back—back—out of danger.

100

Sam Houston: Boy Chieftain
Childhood of Famous
Americans Series
Augusta Stevenson
Illustrated by Paul Laune
Bobbs-Merrill Company
Indianapolis, 1953
Collection of the author

Illustrating the Story

CAN YOU REMEMBER the storybooks you've read without picturing the illustrations? I can't. Sometimes the illustrations in books stay with us as long as the stories themselves. In elementary school, I read and reread *The Childhood of Famous Americans* series of books, intrigued as much by the silhouette-style images as I was interested in the stories. They influenced the choices I made for the illustrations in my storybook on page 78.

In simple storybooks, illustrations hold the attention of the nonreader; in more complex books, they may set the stage for the words on the pages that follow. The pictures add other layers to the story being told. What the words might not fully express, the pictures do. It's hard to imagine gleefully reading Dr. Seuss without the bright illustrations; they shape the way we "picture" the story.

Choosing the manner in which we present the imagery is an important step in the creative process. Relax. You don't have to be a consummate draftsman in order to create an image. Each and every one of us is capable of drawing, even if we're uncomfortable with the end results. It doesn't matter if we think the drawing isn't skillful (we've all felt that way); even an awkward stick figure scrawled on a page can serve our purposes.

You don't have to wield a pencil or brush in order to create your illustrations. Use any of your favorite techniques and skills to create illustrations. Andrea Stern's execution of a single page spread is a portion of the storybook she proposed for this book. It illustrates why you shouldn't be tied to traditional means of creating and illustrating a storybook.

Sources of Imagery

If you choose not to draw your illustrations, you're probably wondering just how you will come up with imagery. Lucky for you, we live in a world filled with all manner of ways to create visual imagery.

I have a fat three-ring binder, filled with images I use in my own work: everything from anatomy illustrations (hands and heads, especially) to images of saints and instructional photos. I collect vintage postcards and will purchase a vintage illustrated dictionary at the drop of a hat. Chances are you have similar material based on your personal preferences—vintage photographs, postcards, magazines, and more. I don't feel guilty stripping out-of-print books of their images and using them. I use the originals when I feel it's important to the integrity of the project, and as my pile of originals dwindles, I resort to photocopies.

Clip art offers a wealth of imagery to choose from. There are online sources for clip art and published books filled with copyright-free imagery. Rubber-stamp imagery is simply astounding in its variety. If shopping in antique malls or dusty shops for vintage material doesn't appeal to you, many companies market facsimiles of vintage imagery. And don't forget those family photographs stored in shoeboxes, albums, or snapshots on your cellphone.

The sources for imagery are limitless. Here's a question: Is it okay to use the imagery you clipped from a magazine, found online, or in an out-of-print book? Like all of life's crucial questions, the answer is not cut-and-dried.

THE VERY PICKY BUTTERFLY

ARTIST
Andrea Stern

Andrea chose one of Hans Christian Andersen's lesser-known tales as her story. It's the story of a butterfly who was in search of a wife among the many flowers that bloom throughout the seasons. He flew from flower to flower through the seasons, but found none of them good enough to be his wife. Eventually he was captured and mounted in a frame, and even while hanging on the wall, he found himself thinking how that houseplant was pretty, but still not quite good enough.

Quilting and stitchery are two of Andrea's skills, so she created a multidimensional illustration with fabric and thread. It's an oversized two-sided page measuring 20 by 16 inches (50.8 by 40.6 cm). Andrea drew her inspiration for one side from coloring book illustrations and the colorful, sculptural side as if an artistically precocious child had been given a big box of crayons.

The base of the page was created with three layers of fabric—muslin, a floral print, and glitter-speckled tulle. Individual flowers and leaves were cut out and strengthened with heavy-duty interfacing before they were embellished with free-motion machine embroidery. Stems, stamens, and buds were created with wool roving that was sculpturally needle felted. Text was created using machine embroidery.

As you know, copyright is the legal right granted to an artist to exclusive use (including sale, publication, or distribution) of his creative work. In other words, as the creator I can do whatever I want with the work I've created. I may use a vintage or historic image as a component of an illustration, in the same way a writer might use a quote from another author to illustrate an idea or strengthen an argument. If you plan on making multiple copies of your work to sell, I'd advise you to closely examine copyright law.

What's most important, I think, is how you choose imagery for a storybook. First and foremost, the imagery must speak to you. If it doesn't speak to you, it probably won't engage your reader. And don't settle for just any image of a house. Be deliberate in your pursuit of the perfect image. A brick, split-level in the middle of a grassy lawn and an ivy-covered Victorian gingerbread cottage in the woods tell two very different stories.

Once you've gathered up your images, how do you get them into your storybook? You're more than likely familiar with the basic techniques, but in case you've forgotten, here's a basic overview of most of the techniques used in this book.

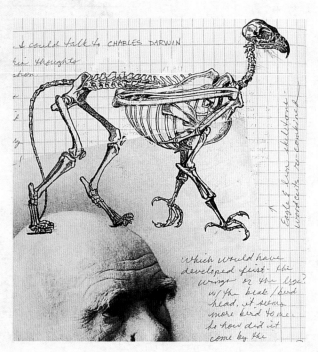

Collage

Collage—simply cutting out an image and adhering it to a surface—is a versatile way to illustrate your storybook. Use the original images or color photocopies. Collaged images are opaque. If you want a transparent or translucent image, you'll need to use a different type of technique.

Rubber Stamping

Rubber stamps are easy to use, but, oh, the sophisticated effects you can achieve with them. Layer images atop one another, mask portions of the image, or use embossing pigments for dimensional effects. Pigment inks, dye-base inks, and solvent-base inks are available in a wide palette of colors. Each ink type has a specific use recommended by the manufacturer and printed on the packaging.

If you can't find the rubber stamp you envision using, choose an image that will suit your needs and take it to a rubber stamp manufacturer (usually your local sign shop). For a nominal cost, they will make a custom-sized stamp for you.

For an original handcrafted appearance, create your own one-of-a-kind rubber stamp. You'll find all of the materials you'll need—soft, vinyl printing blocks and linoleum gouges—in a craft or art supply store. Simply sketch or transfer an image to the block, and carve away portions of the block that you don't wish to print.

I love working with the solvent transfer technique. I've gotten my best results using sturdy, smooth-surfaced papers, but I've also used the technique on tissue paper, fabric, and wood.

~ Terry Taylor

Using Your Computer

I have to admit that I don't use the computer as effectively as it can be used: I'm only somewhat comfortable with my word processing program. I can scan and photocopy images, but beyond that I'm clueless. I do know that various programs exist to manipulate images, compose and kern text, and then combine all of those elements in a layout.

If you're familiar with computer programs and know how to use them, by all means do so. Call me a Luddite, but I prefer the physical processes of cutting and pasting, stitching and painting. Lisa Cook proposed creating a storybook based on a Hans Christian Andersen tale. She used some basic techniques of an image manipulation program to create components for a unique book cover.

Solvent Transfers

Black-and-white photocopies and clay-based (slick) magazine pages transfer to absorbent surfaces using the solvent transfer technique. The solvent breaks down the toners and inks on the paper and transfers the image to the surface. Images transferred with this technique have a soft, transparent, and painterly

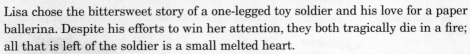

THE STEADFAST TIN SOLDIER

ARTIST
Lisa Cook

Lisa chose the bittersweet story of a one-legged toy soldier and his love for a paper ballerina. Despite his efforts to win her attention, they both tragically die in a fire; all that is left of the soldier is a small melted heart.

The base of the cover is a piece of fabric-covered cardstock. Lisa trimmed a vintage image of a dancer and glued it to one side of the cardstock, and then embellished it with tiny velvet flowers.

Using her computer, Lisa scanned a vintage tintype of a Civil War soldier and then manipulated the image to erase one of his legs. She printed the image and trimmed it to fit the cardstock. Text was created with the computer, including the arching part of the title that curves over the soldier's head. Additional trims— tiny rickrack and a small tag—were attached to the cardstock.

Lisa cut a sheet of mica to size and split the layers in order to cover both sides. She lightly glued the edges of the mica to the covered cardstock.

Using a technique borrowed from stained glass crafting, Lisa applied copper foil tape to the edges and formed loops with the foil around the ink pen. She applied flux to the foil and used a soldering iron to flow solder onto the foil. Afterwards, Lisa patinated the soldered surface to create the aged color. Finally, Lisa added ribbons and a small, metal heart to the pen.

Karen Shelton

appearance. This transfer technique isn't foolproof: results vary depending on the type of image and solvents used. Line drawings transfer more clearly than photographs. Keep in mind that you'll need to create a mirror image copy if your image contains text or if you want your image oriented in a certain direction.

There are many different solvents to use. Some solvents—acetone, toluene-based markers, and lighter fluid—require adequate ventilation when you use them. Nontoxic solvents include oil of wintergreen and citrus-based cleaning solvents.

The transfer process is straightforward. Lay your image facedown and lightly coat the reverse of the image with the solvent of your choice. Burnish or rub the paper with a bone folder, spoon, or similar tool. As you work, periodically lift a corner of the image to check the transfer progress.

Heat Transfers

These transfer papers allow you to transfer an image you've printed on them onto a surface—such as fabric—using heat. Most copy shops will make heat

transfers for you. You can also find heat transfer papers for your home or office ink-jet printer; simply follow the manufacturer's instructions to apply the image. Heat transfers are best suited for fabric but can be used on paper.

Acrylic Medium Transfers

You can create translucent transfers by applying acrylic mediums to photocopied images. Tape an image to a piece of glass. Brush the image with successive coats of acrylic medium, letting each coat dry before applying the next. Anywhere from five to 12 coats may be applied. The more coats you apply, the thicker your transfer will be.

After the layers of medium are thoroughly dry, remove the taped image from the glass. Soak the coated image in water and peel off the paper backing. Use your fingers or a sponge to roll the remaining layers of paper from the transfer. Don't rub too vigorously—the moist transfer will easily stretch or tear. Adhere the image to the page with acrylic medium.

Creating the Text

THE EASIEST WAY to add text to your storybook is to simply write it yourself using pens, pencils, or any other writing tool. This conveys a sense of immediacy and adds a handcrafted touch. However, many people view their handwriting in the same way they feel about their ability to draw. Here are some options you can use to add text to your storybook.

There are many styles and sizes of rubber stamp alphabets in the world. In addition, you can find foreign alphabets if you're writing a story in, let's say, ancient Greek. Use clippings from printed texts, transfer lettering, stickers, metal letters, and labels to create the text of your storybook. Word processing programs on your computer have many different fonts to choose from, and you can print out the text in any size and in any format from strictly horizontal to meandering, curved lines.

You can also use various transfer techniques to add text to a page. The only thing to remember is that if you are using a transfer technique that is placed facedown (heat transfers, solvent transfers, and some water slide transfers), your text will be reversed. Reversed text can be intriguing visually, but it might make it difficult to read your story.

Useful Tools & Materials

Call yourself a crafter, an artist, a dabbler, or what you will. You've got plenty of tools and materials to work with already on hand. Here are the things I find to be indispensable when working on a storybook.

Pencils (or pens if you prefer) are practical and versatile tools for sketching, writing, and mark-making of all sorts. I can't work without my favorite brand of pencil, and I'm sure you've got one too. Keep both graphite and colored pencils on hand, along with your favorite pens.

Each time she did so a pretty little bird would come to her and tell her what she needed to know.

Rubber cement eventually soaks through and discolors the paper. I used it on some pages, knowing that over time it will become more aged. I think it adds to the "patina."

~ Amy Blandford

A bone folder is the perfect tool for crisply creasing folded pages or burnishing. If you don't own one, use the back of a spoon or comb, or the dull side of a table knife. You also can use wooden or hard plastic pottery tools.

It's wonderful to have a large selection of papers, but it can also be overwhelming. Buying paper—like buying fabric or yarn—is a harmless hobby. You can rationalize and say you can never have too much paper, but it's an addiction many of us struggle with. Any type of paper can be used in a storybook: Asian papers, handmade papers, translucent vellums, patterned scrapbook papers, and more. And don't forget how useful recycled papers—charming tea labels, foil wrappers, or chopstick envelopes—can be when you need to achieve a specific look.

Stock up on a variety of tape. In addition to cellophane tape, be sure you have masking and clear packing tape. Masking tape is useful for protecting areas from paint, and packing tape can be used to create image transfers (see page 24). Double-sided tapes are useful for a variety of taping jobs.

Keep adhesives—from an all-purpose white glue to two-step epoxies—in your tool kit:

• White glue will work for most jobs; it's water soluble, clear drying, and you can use it on almost all surfaces from paper to ceramics and fabric to wood.

• Acrylic mediums can be used as a glue with paper and other porous surfaces.

• Hot glues bond quickly and are perfect for attaching uneven surfaces, but limit their use with paper.

• Industrial strength adhesives—two-part epoxy, jewelry glues, silicone glues, and contact adhesives—are especially helpful when you're working with unusual materials such as metal, glass, and plastics.

• Spray adhesives are time-savers; they can be applied to large areas and dry quickly.

• Rubber cement is useful where easy and damage-free removal of adhesive is important.

ONCE
upon a time...

SNUGGLE UNDER A COVERLET OR SETTLE into that sunny place where you love to curl up with a good book. On the following pages you'll find true tales and richly imagined stories, complete with princesses and Mayan kings. Here are the artful storybooks you've been waiting for. May they lead you to faraway lands and then back to your workroom, where I hope you'll be inspired to create your own.

Into the Woods with Hansel & Gretel

Terry Garrett offers a new definition of the traditional storybook with this three-dimensional take on Hansel and Gretel. The accordion-style book inside the box tells the story using collaged images and photos while the exterior of the house prepares the reader for a trip "into the woods."

ARTIST
Terry Garrett

Finished Dimensions
House, 8 x 5 x 4 inches (20.3 x 12.7 x 10.2 cm)
Booklet, 5½ x 4 x ¾ inch (14 x 10.2 x 1.9 cm)
(closed); 5½ x 72 inches (14 x 183 cm) (open)

When it was noon, Gretel shared her piece of bread with Hansel, who had scattered his along the way. Then they fell asleep and evening passed. They did not wake until it was dark night. When the moon came out they set out, but found no crumbs, for the many birds which fly about the woods and fields had picked them all up.

Working Process

1. Beginning this project was a very natural process for Terry Garrett. He wrote, "I have always loved the house form and have been using this form and shape in my artwork for the past couple of years. I also happen to love making books." Since the witch's house plays such a central role in the story, Terry decided to create a house-shaped book.

First, Terry purchased a wooden house-shaped box to hold an accordion book and primed it with acrylic paint. Once dry, he applied a base color and left the box to dry. Next the crackle medium was applied and allowed to dry, followed by a topcoat of paint.

Materials and Tools

Wooden house-shaped box

Crackle medium

Soft gel medium

Found objects

Ephemera & vintage clip art

Altered photographs

Printed text

Heavy black paper

Adhesive laminating machine

2. Terry downloaded the story of *Hansel and Gretel.* Using the story as a guide, he searched his photographic images for backgrounds for the book's pages and collage elements for the box's exterior.

He spent a long time selecting images for the discrete parts of the story. He wrote that he enjoyed "not being bound to a certain historical period for this story. I chose to have few human or character images in my story illustrations, permitting the reader more opportunity to visualize what they want the characters to look like and adding an interactive element to the project."

Some of the images were reduced and printed in black and white for an old "snap shot" look. Many of his photographs were altered using image-editing software.

3. Terry collaged the box with found objects, ephemera, and vintage clip art, using soft gel medium as adhesive.

4. Terry made the accordion book using heavy black paper that was first joined together to create a strip that would be long enough for his story. To cut the background images that appear on each page, Terry

Front, unfolded

used a house-shaped template. He used another smaller template to cut the photographs.

5. A laminated adhesive was used to attach the photographs and images to the book pages. Terry took special care to keep any errant adhesive from causing the pages to stick together.

6. The story text was printed out in a font small enough for the book pages. After tearing out the text, Terry added the excerpts to the pages, along with some clip art to serve as illustrations.

7. Finally, Terry placed the completed book inside the house-shaped box. The roof was made to be removed easily to access the book inside, adding an interactive element to the reader's experience of the book.

TIP: Terry sprinkles ordinary baby powder onto the edge of glued materials and then rubs the powder off to remove any residual adhesive.

Then a soft voice cried from the parlor: "Nibble, nibble, gnaw, Who is nibbling at my house?"

The children went on eating without disturbing themselves. Suddenly the door opened, and a woman came creeping out. She said: "Do come in and stay with me! No harm shall happen to you."

The old woman had only pretended to be so kind; she was in reality a wicked witch. Early in the morning she seized Hansel and carried him to a little stable, and locked him in.

"Silly goose," said the old woman. "The door is big enough; just look, I can get in myself!" The Gretel gave her a push that drove her far into it, and shut the iron door, and fastened the bolt. Gretel ran away and the godless witch was burnt to death.

Gretel ran like lightning to Hansel, opened his stable and cried: "Hansel, we are saved! The old witch is dead!" And as they had no longer any need to fear her, they went into the witch's house, and in every corner there stood chests full of pearls and jewels. "These are far better than pebbles and they trust many of them into their pockets.

When they had walked for two hours they came to a great stretch of water. "We cannot cross," said Hansel, "I see no foot-plank, and no bridge."

Back, unfolded

STORY SUMMARY

When Hansel and Gretel's family can no longer produce enough bread to eat, their parents send them deep into the forest. Using Hansel's trail of shiny pebbles, the children are able to find their way back. However, when hard times fall again, the two are sent into the forest for a second time, and their trail of breadcrumbs is eaten by hungry birds.

While in the forest, Hansel and Gretel happen upon a kindly old woman with a house made of sweets. She lures the children into her house and traps them, with plans to eat the siblings as soon as they are fattened up. Before the woman can begin her meal preparations, Gretel pushes her into the oven and seals the door. With pockets full of gems from the old woman's house, Gretel and Hansel escape to a happy reunion with their parents.

Knitting Is the
Passion of Sarah Flocks

Using an inspiring array of colors, textures, and embellishments, as well as a variety of crafting techniques, Sharon Mann's charming storybook tells a tale that is sure to warm any sock aficionado's heart.

ARTIST
Sharon Mann

Finished Dimensions
9 x 9 inches (22.9 x 22.9 cm)

Working Process

1. Five years ago, while a member of a writing and illustration group, Sharon Mann wrote the poem "Knitting Is the Passion of Sarah Flocks." "The poem has been waiting to be published, and I've always envisioned the poem in a book made of fabric with all the trimmings," said Sharon. "The right venue never came along until this project."

With her poem in hand, Sharon began constructing this book by tracing her drawings onto muslin pages using a colored pencil. She then pinned felt on the back of the muslin and stitched around each square with embroidery thread, using a different color thread for each page.

2. Using a variety of threads, Sharon embroidered around the drawings on each page. She used a variety of stitches and plenty of fun embellishments, from cotton pearls to fancy yarns. To color Sarah, her socks, and her cat, Sharon used watercolors, colored pencils, crayons, and felt.

Sharon knit three socks used on the second page; on other pages she used felt or cut apart purchased socks to create even tinier socks.

3. To build the page borders, Sharon cut four strips of fabric and attached them around each edge. For fun, try using different fabric colors for each page.

4. Sharon created the back cover by pinning together one square piece of colorful fabric and a slightly smaller square of felt, centering the felt on the back of the fabric. She cut out two pieces of fabric to make the pocket and sewed them together with right sides facing, leaving one side open. She turned the pocket right side out and sewed the open side together. Sharon used the same process to create the pocket's flap. She attached both the pocket and the flap to the center of the back cover, adding beads, buttons, and decorative trim.

Materials and Tools

White muslin

White felt

Watercolors

Colored pencils, crayons, and fabric markers

Colorful fabrics

Embroidery and sewing threads

Yarn

Beads, sequins, buttons, and charms

Small clothespins

Red, blue, green, and striped infant socks (or make your own)

There are **socks** on her cat and socks piled on the floor.

In her cozy **green** chair with her cat by her side.

Sarah Flocks' needles click and glide.

Knitting one sock... then two with no time to eat.

Sarah Flocks' passion is really her... **FEET!**

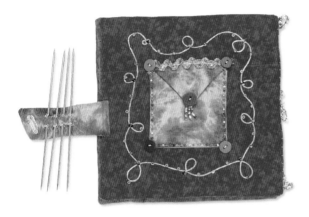

5. Sharon created the latch by sewing two strips of fabric together, leaving one side open. She turned the fabric right side out and then closed the open seam. She created a buttonhole on the left side of the latch and four knitting needle holes at the top and bottom of the latch, finishing each hole with a buttonhole stitch. Finally, she attached the latch to the back cover and sewed a button on the front cover.

6. To get ready for the final steps, Sharon ironed each page from the back and trimmed the edges. She pinned and then stitched the pages together with right sides facing, leaving an open edge. She turned the pages right side out and closed the open side.

7. Sharon then sewed a buttonhole stitch along the left edge of each page and threaded a piece of yarn through the top, middle, and bottom of the button-hole stitches to bind the book. To finish, she tied the yarn binding in a bow.

TIP: Use the pocket on the back cover as a handy holder for your favorite sock pattern.

SARAH'S SOCKS
Want to knit your own socks? Here's the pattern Sarah (and Sharon) used.

Materials
Sock yarn
Needles: set of 4, size 1 (2.25 mm)

Gauge: 8 sts & 10 rows = 1 inch (2.5 cm)

Pattern:
Cast on 36 sts and join in round.
Work 8 rounds K2, P2 rib.

Heel flap:
K18, turn, P18, turn.
Work another 10 rows in Stockinette stitch.

Turn Heel:
K11, SKPO, turn.
P6, P2tog, turn.
K6, SKPO, turn.
Repeat rows 2 and 3 until you work across all heel sts and have 7 left.
Pick up 9 st along edge of heel flap.
K18 across instep, pick up 10 along other edge of heel flap then K the 7 heel sts—44 sts.
K 1 round.
Next round: K6, K2tog, K20, K2tog tbl, K14.
K 1 round.
Next round: K5, K2tog, K20, K2tog tbl, K13.
K 1 round.
Next round: K4, K2tog, K20, K2tog tbl, K12.
K 1 round.
Next round: K3, K2tog, K20, K2tog tbl, K11—36 sts.
K 6 rounds.
Toe: K2tog, K7, repeat around—32 sts.
K 1 round.
K2tog, K6, repeat around—28 sts.
K 1 round.
Continue decreasing until there are 8 sts. Cut yarn and thread in and out of stitches. Pull up tight and fasten off. Weave in loose yarn.

The Queen of Tarts

Vive la reine! Catherine Moore is well-known for her paper doll designs.
Her storybook artfully blends the paper doll form with a book format to create lushly
embellished, lightly gilded tableaux vivant from the life of Marie Antoinette.

ARTIST
Catherine Moore

Finished Dimensions
16 x 8 inches (40.6 x 20.3 cm)

Materials and Tools

Chipboard mannequin form

Drawing paper

130 lb watercolor paper

Gel matte medium

Mat board

Muslin or bookcloth

Copyright-free images

Assortment of acrylic paints,
colored pencils, and pastels

Decorative stencils

Ledger and printed book pages

Spray adhesive

Patterned papers

Awl

Waxed linen bookbinding thread

Passementerie—an assortment of
ribbons, trims and millinery flowers,
buttons, and beads

Acrylic gesso

One small eyehook

Working Process

1. Catherine avers that "dreaming it (the book) was simple, engineering it was more challenging." She used a chipboard mannequin form to create a substantial support and stand for the book. The size of the book pages was determined by the size of the mannequin she chose.

To give the mannequin a form closer to the tightly corseted silhouette of the eighteenth century, Catherine cut the waistline of the mannequin. Once the waistline was trimmed, Catherine sketched a pannier (skirt or petticoat worn in the late 1700s). She used the sketch to create a template for the storybook's cover and pages.

A simple way to make the pannier template symmetrical is to fold the sketched shape in half, then cut the shape out. When you unfold the shape, you will have a symmetrical pattern.

2. The physical structure of Catherine's book is unusual. The front and back cover are a single piece. The pages are six-paneled concertinas, one for each half of the pannier. The front cover is a single piece. Catherine measured the width of the pannier and divided it in half to determine the width needed for a single page. She measured and marked the watercolor paper three times the length needed to create a single page. Using a bone folder, she scored and folded a three-panel unit.

Next, Catherine used the pannier shape as a template to mark the folded unit. She used a sharp craft knife to trim the shape of the folded panel.

Catherine created three additional units in the same manner.

3. Catherine cut 1-inch (2.5 cm) strips of watercolor paper, and set them aside. She laid two units end to end, and adhered a strip of paper where the two units met. This created a six-page concertina panel. She repeated the process to create a second panel.

4. Catherine then had two 6-paneled concertinas, one with a left- and the other with a right-sided perspective. Catherine wanted the book to open toward the center so it mimicked the full-skirted effect of the pannier. To keep the folds in the center of the skirt from unfolding, she brushed a thin layer of gel matt medium along a ½-inch (1.3 cm) margin at the edge of the panels.

5. Catherine created the front and back covers using matt board. She marked the board using the pannier template, and cut it out with a sharp craft knife. She marked and cut out a second shape.

To create the front cover, Catherine marked a line down the center of one of the shapes. She marked a ¼-inch (6 mm) gap centered on the line, then cut along the two lines. The gap created allows the book to open along the centerline.

6. Using the uncut board shape as a template, Catherine marked and cut out two pannier shapes from watercolor paper.

Next, she cut two strips of bookcloth. Catherine adhered each strip of cloth centered on the wrong side of both pannier shapes to reinforce areas to be bound. Once the adhesive on the back of the front cover dried, she scored down the center fold.

7. Catherine finds it easier to illustrate the pages of a book before binding it. It allows you more freedom to work on the pages flat than to work around bound pages.

Two basic image formats illustrate the story. Like many mixed-media artists, Catherine is a collector of

antiquarian books and has a collection of very old engravings to draw from. She scanned and printed imagery onto sketch paper, and hand-colored the imagery with pencils.

She also used hand-drawn and commercial silhouettes. The silhouette of Marie Antoinette as a child was block printed using a hand-carved rubber stamp. More finely detailed silhouette imagery was printed out and then cut out before painting and collaging them onto the pages.

8. "I love beginning compositions with layers of texture and color," Catherine states. She used stencils and pounced paint techniques to create patterns on some

pages. Other textural backgrounds used include old book pages from French language texts and antique ledger papers onto which she further developed her compositions with paint, pastels, and collage elements.

9. Rather than use hand-lettering techniques, Catherine created her text using a computer and printing it onto sketch paper. Catherine routinely uses computer-generated and printed elements in her work. To give those printed elements a bit of protection, she uses an acrylic spray fixative on her printouts. Occasionally she will add another bit of protection and rub the sprayed surface with soft, bleached bee's wax.

10. Once the basic imagery and text were added to the pages, Catherine began to assemble the book. She used gel medium to adhere the right and left concertinas to the back cover board, allowing for a ¼-inch (6 mm) margin between the two units. She pressed the pages under a heavy book and allowed them to dry. Before proceeding to the next step in the process, Catherine covered the exposed, unadorned panels with decorative paper.

11. Catherine used an awl to create a hole ½ inch (1.3 cm) down from the center on the back cover and another hole ½ inch (1.3 cm) down from the first hole. She repeated this process from the bottom center.

Catherine used large paper clips to secure the front and back covers together. To facilitate the stitching, she used the awl to make matching holes in the front cover. Then, working from the backside of the back cover, she stitched through the first hole and back out through the second hole before she tied off and trimmed the cords. She repeated the stitching process in the lower two holes.

12. Catherine embellished the front cover with decorative papers and type. To print the type directly onto the decorative paper, she taped the upper edge

of decorative paper onto her printer paper, and then ran the paper through her printer. Additional layers of paper were added to the front cover.

When she was satisfied with the look and composition, Catherine used aerosol glue to attach the cover to the stitched book. As a finishing touch, she added dimensional trims to the front cover. Catherine covered the back cover with decorative papers as well.

13. Catherine painted the mannequin form and base with two layers of white gesso. When dry, she collaged decorative paper to the wrong side of the mannequin form as well as to the base.

She printed the face and torso in brown ink onto buff-colored sketch paper. She reinforced the sketch paper with two layers of watercolor paper and then cut it out with scissors. The wrong side and edges of the doll were painted with flesh-colored paint.

The bodice portion of the dress was cut out of decorative paper and adhered to the mannequin's torso. To create the jointed arms, Catherine cut the arms at the elbow and then reattached them with brads. Finally, the entire torso was glued to the mannequin form using gel medium. Catherine pressed the doll under a heavy book and allowed it to dry before embellishing the doll with dimensional items.

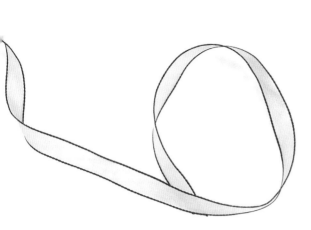

14. The entire book was assembled by using gel medium to adhere the pannier-shaped book to the doll form. Catherine screwed a small eyehook into the back of the chipboard form to anchor the ribbon closure she planned for the front of the book. Catherine stitched antique brass buttons through the front cover and the first concertina panels on each side. She wrapped a length of narrow ribbon around the cover to securely close the book.

15. Not content with simply creating a dimensional book, Catherine carefully packed the book in a decorative box for shipment. No plain brown cardboard would be fit for this queen! In addition, she created a hand-painted and embellished box frame to use for display or for photography.

STORY INSPIRATION

The Austrian born Maria Antonia was betrothed at age 14 and soon after married Louis-Auguste, crown prince of France. Marie's fashion excesses are legendary, as were her elaborate poufs (coiffures), all of which did nothing to endear her to the downtrodden people of France. While as yet mere teens, their coronation took place during a bread shortage, and Marie was infamously misquoted as saying "Let them eat cake." Marie was an attentive mother to her children and enjoyed playing with them on the palace grounds. Among her legendary expenditures is *Le Petit Hameau*, a simulated hamlet in which she and her friends played milk maidens and shepherdesses, but not before the sheep and cows were bathed and perfumed for their roles. Her excessive expenses are considered by some to be her chief crime, but she had no sense of it. She was executed by guillotine at the age of 38, at the height of the French Revolution.

A Trip to the Lake

This lovely little storybook tells the story of two sisters, Ethel and Edith, and an adventure at their aunt and uncle's house on the lake. Jane Reeves used black-and-white images paired with photocopies of vintage postcards, complete with handwritten notes to the girls' parents, to fashion this tale of lakeside escapades.

ARTIST
Jane Reeves

Finished Dimensions
4½ x 6¼ inches (11.4 x 15.9 cm) (closed)
32 x 6¼ inches (81.3 x 15.9 cm) (open)

Working Process

1. Jane's storybook began with 16 vintage postcards and a variety of old photos and magazine illustrations; the story, and the ever-delightful duo of Edith and Ethel, came later.

2. Jane pictured creating a folder of postcards. Postcard folders are easily found in antique shops and online. Jane started cutting strips of cardstock a little over 6 inches (15.2 cm) wide. She joined these strips to make a single longer strip. Using an accordion fold, she divided this piece into eight sections, leaving a flap at one end.

Materials and Tools

Cardstock

Old postcards

Vintage photos and images

Tissue paper

Glue stick

Vacation Greetings

May splendid opportunities
For rest and gay diversions
Make your vacation trip the most
Delightful of excursions.

ST CLUB, BUCKEYE LAKE.

STORY SUMMARY

Sisters Ethel and Edith travel to the lake to visit their beloved Aunt Ruth and Uncle Walt. Sunset cruises, visits to the nearby bathing beach, and a lakeside dance complete their summer fun. Although Ethel becomes momentarily distracted and then devastated by the dapper Fred, a boat ride with Uncle Walt quickly revives her. Having learned their lesson, Ethel and Edith return home, wiser now and with their friendship renewed.

3. She created a template based on a vintage postcard folder. Next, she traced around the template and cut her cover from cardstock, folding it to create the basic envelope shape.

4. Jane photocopied 16 postcards and glued one to each side of the accordion.

5. She worked on creating Ethel and Edith, and their cohorts, using an assortment of vintage images like antique cars, flowers, and fish. To highlight the images, she drew in details with a fine-point marker and glued them in place on each panel. Then, to create the text for the book, Jane wrote sections of the story on tissue paper and glued the tissue paper to the appropriate pages.

6. Jane embellished the cover using postcards and other images. She also created a title for the book on her computer and glued it to the front cover. To give the folder a vintage look, she used paint and ink to distress both the pages and cover. Assembly was simple: she glued the accordion's flap to the inside of the postcard cover.

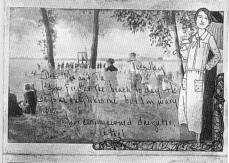

Coyote and the Lizard People

A six-month stint in Arizona deepened Lisa Glicksman's interest in Native American cultures and myths. Back at home, she began experimenting with sand painting techniques and created this charming storybook.

ARTIST
Lisa Glicksman

Finished Dimensions
8¼ x 6⅜ inches (21 x 16.1 cm)

Coyote spies on the lizard people playing a game.

Materials and Tools

Bound sketchbook

Paper

Artist's crayons

Spray fixative

Double adhesive film

Stickpin

Colored sand

Film canisters

Wide soft brush
(for whisking sand away)

Copper foil

Acrylic paints

Fabric

Stencil film

Decorative, textured paper

Working Process

1. Lisa strengthened the sketchbook pages by gluing the pages together (see page 16). She then painted the pages with acrylics and allowed them to dry. For rich saturated color, Lisa applied several coats of paint.

2. To create the backgrounds for the sand paintings, Lisa tore pieces of black paper into irregular shapes. Then she rubbed crayons on the paper and sealed it with a coat of spray fixative.

3. Lisa drew the design for the sand paintings on double adhesive film. She used a stickpin to separate the layers of film, and pried off the first layer of backing. Next, she affixed the film to the black paper, and then peeled off the top layer with her original drawing. She then cut out each shape, and reapplied it to the film, leaving the area for the first sand application exposed.

TIP: Not all double adhesive films are created equal. Lisa recommends finding one that has a backing that you can draw on, and has a clear, not translucent, film.

4. For easier handling, Lisa transferred the colored sand into film canisters and sprinkled it onto the adhesive film. Excess sand was whisked away with a soft brush onto a creased piece of paper, and then funneled back into the film canister. She continued to peel off the backing for each separate color until the image was completely filled in with sand. To achieve a softer, blended look, Lisa mixed some of the colored sand together before applying it to the desired area.

5. For additional detailing, Lisa used acrylic paint applied with a fine brush. When each sand painting was finished, she sprayed it with a fixative.

6. Lisa printed the story and tore out individual captions to create textured edges. Then she mounted the captions to the black paper with glue.

7. For an engraved look, she incised the storybook title on a piece of copper foil. To add a bit of patina to the copper, she applied a coat of acrylic paint, and used a soft cloth to remove most of the paint.

8. Lisa stenciled some animal track designs on thin fabric. A zigzag line of stitching was added for embellishment before she cut the fabric to fit both front and back covers. Lisa cut a panel of textured paper slightly smaller than her copper foil title. She then affixed the edges of the foil to the reverse side of the paper. Both cloth and paper were secured to the covers with glue.

TIP: Embossing powders or glitter can be used to create a similar effect but are more challenging to work with than sand.

Elder Lizard says, "Much as I don't like Coyote, we can't let him die merely because he tried to play our game. We must revive him."

The lizards bring out their magic potions and revive Coyote.

Coyote's life is restored. He dashes home fast as lightning.

STORY SUMMARY

Coyote is intrigued by the Lizard People's game. He attempts to try it himself and is smashed to pieces by the rocks. The Elder Lizard takes pity on Coyote and magically revives him. With his life restored, Coyote dashes off home.

China Ranch
(A Secret in the Desert)

A day traveling through a remote desert brings unexpected surprises in this colorful storybook by Linda Trenholm. When Linda proposed the story, we serendipitously discovered that we had both visited this charming spot located near Death Valley. A collection of novel imagery and a unique antiqued finish bring this enchanting story to life on the page.

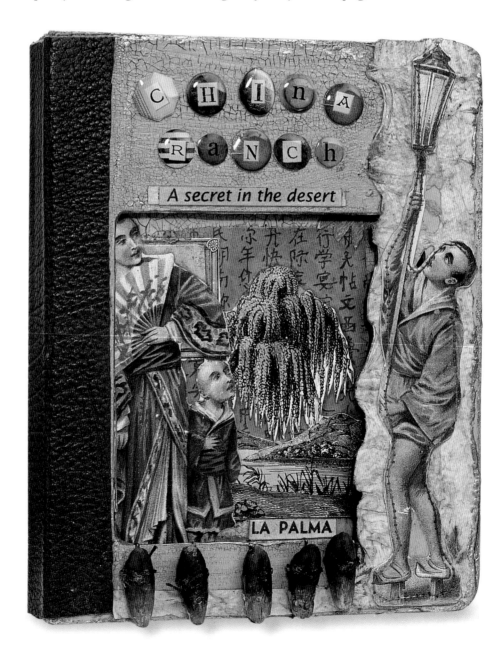

ARTIST
Linda Trenholm

Finished Dimensions
6⅝ x 5¼ inches (16.8 x 13.3 cm)

On the road so long and steep

LA PALMA

We came upon the Date Palm trees.

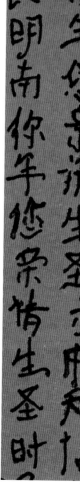

Materials and Tools

Board book

Sandpaper

Gesso

Matte acrylic medium

Crackle medium

Ink

Water-soluble oil pastels

Decorative paper, die cuts, tissue, and fabric

Postage stamps and postcards

Rubber stamps, ink pad, and embossing powder

Various embellishments: rhinestones, beads, buttons, ribbon, and found objects

Waxed thread

Leather

Gel medium

Wax sealant

Working Process

1. This storybook began life as a board book. Linda first removed the glossy finish on each page (see page 16). She then applied several layers of gesso, letting each coat dry before adding the next. To prevent the pages from sticking together during the drying process, Linda set the book upright and spread the pages open.

2. Before she began to create the pages, Linda developed a rough layout for each spread, loosely arranging her images and papers and deciding what color palette she would use.

3. Linda painted each page with two coats of acrylic paint mixed with matte medium. She allowed each coat to dry before she applied a final coat of crackle medium. Ink washes were applied to some of the pages and then wiped off with a cloth after a few minutes to achieve a subtler surface. To emphasize the texture of the pages, Linda applied water-soluble oil pastels, rubbing the color into the cracks. She then removed the remaining color with a damp cloth to create a nice, antique finish.

Shaped like
my umbrella
they grew

PALMIER. — Les palmiers sont une famille d'arbres de
haute taille couronnés à leur sommet par un faisceau
de larges feuilles dites palmes. Le plus important des
palmiers est le dattier, qui produit les fruits sucrés ap-
pelés dattes.

Towering high

through the sky of blue.

This truck we'll us

CHINA
BRANCH
DATES

With mounds of swe

our crates

asty dates.

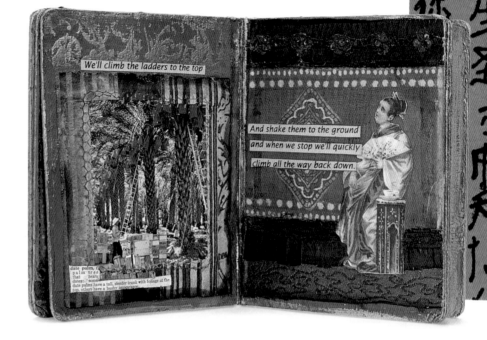

We'll climb the ladders to the top

And shake them to the ground
and when we stop we'll quickly
climb all the way back down.

4. Once her pages were prepared, Linda began layering the surfaces, applying paper, torn tissue, and fabric using gel medium. She glued her images to these layered surfaces. To create additional patterns and textures, Linda used a number of rubber stamping and embossing techniques. She then attached a variety of found objects and embellishments to complete each page.

5. Once the illustrations were complete, Linda composed and printed the text using her computer. After gluing down the text, Linda finished each page by rubbing bronze paint along the edges. For a subtle sheen and added protection, Linda rubbed wax onto each page. She allowed the wax to dry overnight and then used a soft cloth to buff the pages.

6. As a final touch, Linda embellished her board book binding by cutting a strip of leather that she applied to the spine using gel medium. She created the binding by attaching a premeasured strip of leather and using gel medium to secure it.

Soon off we go. It's time for lunch.

Good-Bye my China Ranch.

We make our way, it's not too far.

A gourmet lunch we'll eat.

Café C'est Si Bon
MIRACLE IN THE DESERT
[Solar-Internet Café]
Espresso
Vegetarian Gourmet Food
Crepes
Baked Goods
Cheeses and more
HOST & Owner- David
OPEN 7am to 5pm daily
Closed only on Tues.
Highway 127, #118
P.O.Box 37
Shoshone, Ca. 92384
Tel. # (760)852-4307
DavidWash@earth...

Café Cest Si Bon,
a special place, where every meals a treat.

STORY SUMMARY

On a long journey through the desert, a group of travelers happen upon an enchanted grove of date palm trees. They quickly make plans to harvest the sweet fruits by climbing the trees and shaking the dates free. The travelers happily share their harvest with a flock of birds and then pause for a moment of rest after their labors. They soon continue their journey refreshed and revived, with plans for a gourmet lunch at a special café.

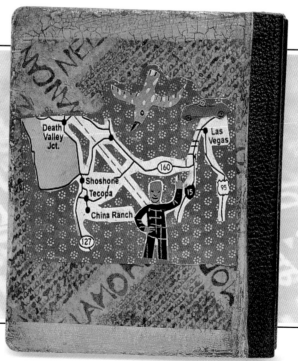

Hunter's 10th Birthday

Inspired by a special family member, this storybook uses photos and metal-framed chipboard pages to tell the story of a fabulous birthday celebration. Creator Erikia Ghumm confesses that "we always have a party for my dog with a doggie cake and presents," although she admits "it's kind of silly."

ARTIST
Erikia Ghumm

Finished Dimensions
6⅜ x 6⅜ inches (16.2 x 16.2 cm)

Hunter's 10th Birthday by Erikia Ghumm

Materials and Tools

Photo paper

Chipboard

Acrylic and spray paints

Cardstock

Round foam stamp

Patterned papers

Number stencils

Spray and glass glitter

Spray adhesive

Metal tape

Metal embossing wheel

Vintage book covers

Photo corners

Can lid

Liquid glue

Binder rings

Ribbon

Working Process

1. Erikia wrote that her "inspiration for this book came from a special childhood storybook that was given to me by my grandma. It was a personalized book with a story about me and my family, and I loved reading it!" As an artist, Erikia keeps these childhood storybooks close to her heart and her workshop, perusing their pages whenever she needs inspiration.

To create her own personalized storybook, Erikia started by manipulating photos with photo-editing software and then printing them out onto ink-jet photo paper.

2. Erikia cut chipboard into squares to use as the base for her pages.

3. Erikia then painted cardstock with acrylic and spray paints. When the papers were dry, she used a foam stamp and more acrylic paint to create patterns on the pages. In addition, she embellished various patterned papers, applying contrasting colors of spray paint along the edges. She used stencils and spray paint to add numbers to the papers.

Today is the day, a very big day:

It is Hunter's 10th Birthday!

A big party was planned and it was so grand;

All who attended said it was splendid.

They served up a cake made from potato and meat;

It was just right for Hunter to eat.

The next event did cause such a stir;

The opening of gifts that were made out of fur.

4. For extra color and texture, Erikia added a final layer of spray glitter to all the papers. She adhered the papers to the chipboard squares using spray adhesive. As a final flourish, she applied metal tape around the edges of the chipboard pages, rubbing over the tape with a bone folder. Using an embossing wheel, she rolled over all of the tape's edges, giving it a dot pattern. To enhance the pattern, she applied black acrylic paint and wiped away the excess with a paper towel.

5. To create the front and back covers, Erikia cut vintage book covers into squares, using the book's pages as a size guide. Erikia liked the look of the vintage book covers, which give the project the look and feel of a real book. She then punched holes in the chipboard pages and the covers with a hole punch.

When the party was over, he grinned ear to ear;
It was such fun; we can't wait 'til next year!

The End

Photos taken: February 28, 2006

Book created: July 31, 2007

STORY SUMMARY

Hunter, a black dog with expressive eyes, celebrates his 10th birthday with a grand affair. With plenty of friends to join him, oodles of presents to open, and his very own cake to devour, Hunter is one happy camper.

6. Erikia used a computer to generate text for the book and then printed her story onto cardstock. She trimmed the text to fit onto the pages. Next, she added her photos to the pages with photo corners and added the cutout text below the pictures.

7. Erikia created a medallion for the front cover by embellishing a small lid with spray-painted patterned paper and glass glitter. She added the title of the book, adhering it to the interior of the decorated lid. Finally, Erikia bound the book with the binder rings adorned with scraps of ribbon as a final decorative touch.

A Story of Resignation

About this project, Susan McBride wrote, "Quitting a job can be a life-changing event. To be politically correct or to burn a bridge...that is the question." Her tiny storybook, made from a matchbook, explores those feelings through visuals and a resignation form letter.

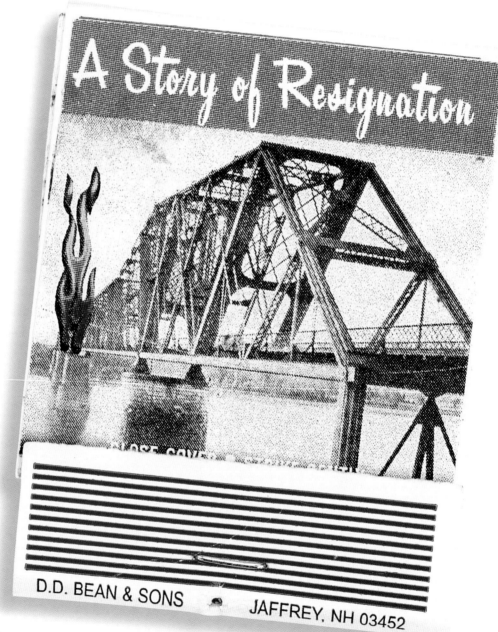

ARTIST
Susan McBride

Finished Dimensions
2 x 1½ inches (5 x 3.8 cm) (closed)
9½ x 1½ inches (24.1 x 3.8 cm) (open)

Materials and Tools

Matchbook
Several low-resolution images
Printer paper
Spray adhesive

Working Process

1. Susan found her form-letter text on a business advice website, in the "heart-felt" category. She admits that she "found it amusing that people seek reference for writing heartfelt missives."

2. She designed the book's cover and pages using computer layout and design software. Susan used low-resolution image files to accompany the form-letter text, which was set in a distressed typewriter font.

3. Susan printed the interior pages on a color printer. She used a craft knife to cut out the design and then glued the strip to the inside of the front cover of the matchbook with spray adhesive.

4. Next, Susan folded the interior pages of the storybook using an accordion fold.

5. She printed the cover images and cut out the designs using a craft knife. Using spray adhesive, she attached the images to the front and back covers of the matchbook.

STORY SUMMARY

Dear Sir or Madame,
I am writing you to officially tender my resignation from ___ effective Friday, June 15th.

Working for ___ has been a wonderful experience. I could not ask for a better group of colleagues. I have grown in many ways here and will always treasure the opportunities provided for me by ___.

I will be accepting a position as an ___ with ___. While I will miss my friends here at ___, I feel that it is time for a new challenge and experience.

If you have any questions, please feel free to ask.

Best wishes,

___

Field Journal—Birds of Prey
The Gryphon Journal

This is a storybook for the obsessive (in the most positive sense of the word) grown-up. Amy's rigorous combination of drawing, choice of ephemera, and detailed story line is a sight to both read and behold. She wrote, "The final book contains maybe a third of the stuff I collected for it."

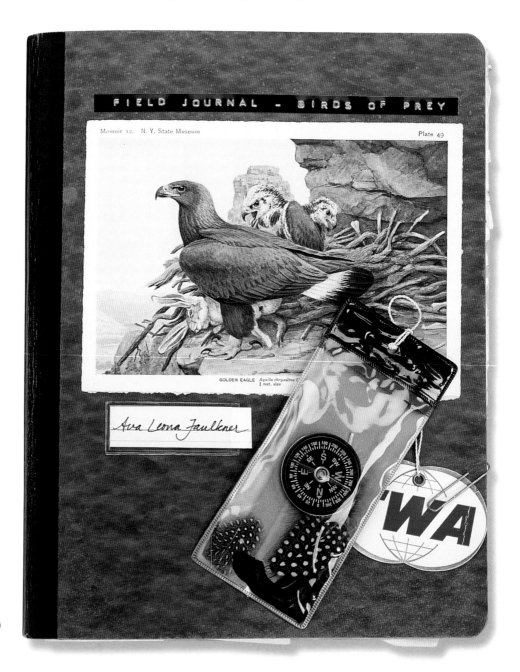

ARTIST
Amy Blandford

Finished Dimensions
11¾ x 9¼ inches (29.8 x 23.5 cm)

Materials and Tools

Composition book with
grid-ruled pages

Ephemera: maps, airline tickets,
postcards, envelopes, pages torn
from old textbooks, etc.

Variety of small notepapers

Feathers

Compass

Small mirror

Vintage photos

Digital photos/public domain web
images

Colored pencils

Colorless blender

Rubber cement

Working Process

1. Amy's idea for re-creating an ornithologist's field journal as the basis of her storybook has a practical side to it. She wanted to archive some of the bird skeleton sketches that she had created over a period of years. At the start, she thought the story would center on a search for the California condor. When she ran across a collection of old plane tickets, boarding passes, and airline stickers, she combined the flight themes and expanded the territory for the story. Like many of us, she admits that "I don't remember when it became about gryphons, maybe when I was cleaning my garage and found the illustration I did in college." That illustration made its way onto the inside front cover.

2. Amy insists that "to create a believable story about something mythical, it's important to have the other details as realistic as possible." She believes that it's important to watch out for anachronisms when illustrating a story. For example, she suggests that you don't set a story "in 1959 in a National Park that didn't exist as such until the 1970s." Such attention to detail is one of the reasons why Amy's book is so engrossing, though Amy avers that "most people wouldn't notice that, but I like things to be accurate."

Not everyone has the time and energy (to say nothing of funds) to try and locate genuine, vintage photos of places and people. Amy admits that some things are "fakes." To that end, she used twenty-first-century computer technology to make new photos look old, taking care to make the dimensions of the prints historically accurate.

The vintage "polaroids" on pages 30, 99, and 119 were created by combining two or more images. Amy used her computer program to convert them to CMYK and desaturated the color. She used a spe-

cial filter to create the grainy effect of old photographs as well.

She also faked other documents, such as the report card on page 97. After scanning the card, Amy erased all the typing, and replaced it with new names, dates, and grades.

3. After doing a bit of research on the history and origins of the gryphon, Amy created a spreadsheet to help her align "nesting sites" with the locations on the travel ephemera she had collected. This helped

her focus the story events in the places that matched up reasonably well with the ephemera. She used the dates on the envelopes and tickets to give shape to her story timeline.

4. Like all writers, Amy made some changes and revisions in the story as she worked on it. At some point, the narrator Amy originally envisioned changed from an ornithology professor to a college student studying birds. One reason for the change is that a professional would use terminology that Amy wasn't

familiar with, and learning enough to make it sound believable was too involved for this project. Amy found it easier to write the story from the viewpoint of a passionate birding novice.

As she worked, Amy started to develop the backstory about the narrator's family to further develop the storyline. In addition, she decided to include lists of bird facts, dates, names of places, and weather reports to make the story more realistic. In some places, these elements are used as design elements.

The journaling sections recount the main narrative, and the other elements on the pages provide additional details that aren't spelled out as clearly. For example, it might seem random that some of the anatomy sketches are drawn on pages from a trigonometry book and Shakespeare's sonnets. A few pages later, you might notice that she's failing or barely passing those subjects—she's drawing in her textbooks instead of paying attention in class.

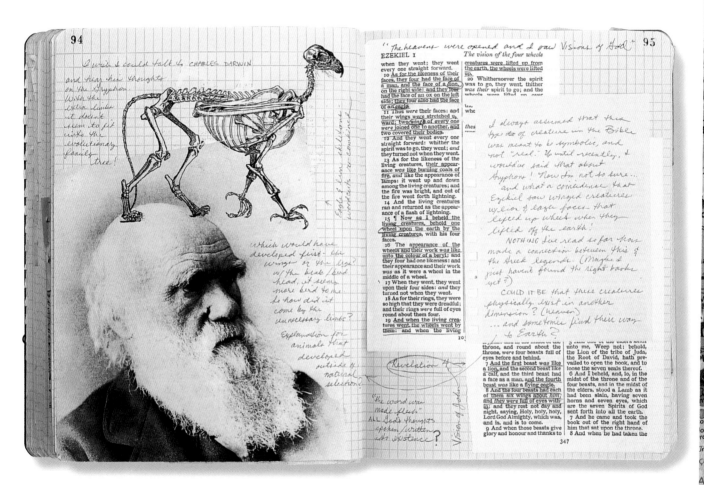

5. Once the story line was developed, Amy began working on the physical structure of the book. Amy likes to organize items on each page first, working from large to small. For example, big maps or photos would be placed first, and any text fit in around it later. On other pages, a block of text might be the largest element. Amy finds that varying the sizes from page to page keeps the whole book visually interesting.

Working with a large amount of ephemeral material, it's easy for a book to become fat and unwieldy.

Amy tore out a page or two as she worked, to compensate for the paper she added .

Amy added elements to the pages with old-fashioned cellophane tape, staples, and rubber cement, as well as using a glue stick. She says, "Glue sticks have always reminded me of those paste pots I used in elementary school, which makes it more historically "correct."

Have been walking North for about 4 hours. It's slow going there, very rocky. Large rocks and small, & a twisted ankle could be deadly out here. NO ONE would even have a CLUE where to look for me, and it would be days or weeks before anyone realized they should!

Okay, now I'm looking for a TREE or a ROCK or something that looks like a "Guardian." Like a guardian angel? The Gryphon itself is a guardian. & the poem talks about TREASURE — so maybe it's a Gryphon guarding gold?

GOLD... I wonder if it's in nugget form? They say the Gryphons dig it up, their beak are strong enough to chomp it out from the rock! Maybe ancient coins that it's stolen from men? Which brings to mind another thought — is it going to be a ruthless murder? It probably already knows that I'm here! I suppose I should be TERRIFIED, but I am NOT going back!

this has to be the
GUARDIAN

the beak, the watchful eye...
"He watches the Treasure."

I guess I'm turning right again! Ahead (to the right) are the biggest hills I've climbed yet! I think I'm officially in the lower Himalayas. I hope it's on this side of the next range of "mountains"!

PROCEED WITH CAUTION!

Running out of daylight again. This is probably NOT a safe place to stop — could try to make it to the hills & find a gap in the rocks, but GOD ONLY KNOWS what might be in there in the dark!

MARCH 6TH 1963
Camped out under the Guardian, hoping he would guard ME, but didn't sleep.
Heading for the hills.

3:40 PM
Have RETREATED to the Guardian tree —

I FOUND THE NEST.

It's huge, way larger than an eagle's nest. 6 feet wide? The size of a big comfy bed, if one dared to lie down in it.
I DIDN'T.
Woven amongst the branches and bramble — hundreds and hundreds of BONES.

Shrike for comparison

Can't tell whose bones (or what's) without more study — ribs, femurs, phalanges... the center is filled with gravel too (not to mention nits on the ground (also not nest-like))

I thought there were two eggs in the center. White, about the size of ostrich eggs — if found me in my tracks, thinking — the Gryphon must be there standing guard! But — no sign of her. After several minutes, I got up the courage to take a closer look, and realized with a SHOCK that the eggs aren't eggs at all, but half-buried human skulls! So just the crown of the head showing through the dust.

I saw her.
She's gorgeous!

I can't even describe what it was like to first see the Gryphon face-to-face — but I have to try to write it down before I forget!
It was TERRIFYING — good thing I'm young or my heart couldn't take it.
I felt that if she were to rip me to shreds, I would completely deserve it.
Then I almost thought that being ripped to shreds by something that beautiful and noble would be an honor.

ANY THOUGHTS I had about retrieving any GOLD completely vanished.
I had gone back to see the nest, somehow not even expecting to see the Gryphon.
I was studying the skulls — definitely human —

STORY SUMMARY

The tale begins with a simple notebook being kept by Ava, a college student, as she studies bird skeletons. She takes it on a bird-watching trip to Alaska and documents a variety of shore birds and eagles. We learn that her father recently died in a plane crash, and that she's very angry at the pilot, who survived. She sees a strange animal that looks like a lion/eagle combo and manages to take its picture (but not a good one).

Back at home, she starts filling the journal with research about gryphons: references in historical literature and art, possible scientific explanations, and how they're physically impossible. A letter comes for her dad (who we deduce might have also been an ornithologist) describing a creature in Russia/Mongolia that was just like the one she saw.

She goes to Mongolia in the dead of winter to find it, with no luck. Reading the mythology of the gryphon, she's intrigued by Nemesis, the goddess of divine retribution. Ava agrees that people should get what they deserve, thinking specifically of the man who was responsible for killing her dad.

The next several pages review all the things gryphons are symbolic of—loyalty, the great opposites, and the dual nature of Christ—including details about the healing power of their feathers. This gryphon obsession continues through the next semester, and Ava has to drop out of most of her classes to avoid failing them. Her report card is a wake-up call; she decides this goose chase has consumed too much of her life.

Two years pass. Helping mom clean out her dad's old office, she finds another letter inside a book. This one has a photo of a gryphon, and a cryptic poem explaining how (or not) to locate its nest. Convinced that this time she can find it, she makes a chart listing the pros and cons of all the areas she's researched. She likes for everything to have a reason, for everything to make sense; she doesn't take it well when they don't.

Based on all the evidence, and a rare gut feeling, she heads for Calcutta. Good choice—when she gets there, she finds the clue to the real location in Sikkim, in the Himalayas. Away she goes, following the clues, dreaming of gold, glory, and revenge, until she finds the gryphon's nest, and then the gryphon. Remarkably, it doesn't kill her. Instead, Ava sees something shiny in the nest. It turns out not to be gold but a small mirror reflecting the sun. Looking into it, she sees the toll the last few years have taken on her. She sees in her expression the ugliness in her own soul— an unforgiving, unmerciful heart and a very self-centered grief. Suddenly she can see the pain of others (like her mother) and recognize her own need for mercy and compassion. She keeps the mirror and a "healing" feather as a reminder of her (spiritual) journey.

A Quartet of Storybooks

To create these delightful books, artist Margert Ann Kruljac used stories written by children because, as she points out, "children are constantly creating tales." Each one is thoughtfully embellished to reflect the personality of its child author, with special papers, ribbon, found objects, and enchanting imagery.

ARTIST
Margert Ann Kruljac

Finished Dimensions
Each: 7 x 7 inches (17.8 x 17.8 cm)

Materials and Tools

Patterned paper

Adhesive

Vintage imagery or images drawn
by children, scanned and printed
onto cardstock

Various embellishments

Children's board books

Found objects

Working Process

1. Margert selected board books for her storybooks. She prepared each book by lightly sanding the pages and cover (see page 16).

2. For each book, Margert considered the personality of its child author, and how best to visually represent their work. *Once Upon A Time* was written by ten-year-old Julia Kruljac, who loves to use found objects in her own art projects and who frequently

expresses herself using symbolism. For this book, using an actual fork to represent "a fork in the road" was exactly what Julia would have done.

3. Margert used a variety of patterned paper and embellishments to embellish the pages.

A friend's six-year-old daughter wrote *The Little Girl* as a homework assignment. To reflect the "girliness" of the author, Margert selected soft-hued patterned papers, embellishments, and imagery.

Another six-year-old wrote *Magical and Me*. For this book Margert printed Hayley's handwriting on

patterned paper and enhanced her original peacock drawing by scanning and manipulating the image with her computer. Dimensional embellishments were added to each of the pages.

Ode to the Planets was written by a seven-year-old as a poetry assignment for school. To create the background, Margert used swatches from wallpaper. She used adhesive lettering and rubber stamping on the pages. The poem's text is rubber stamped in a simple font and then heat embossed.

ode to the planets

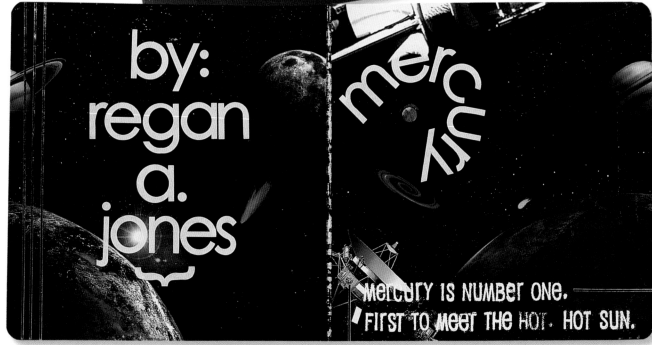

by:
regan
a.
jones

mercury

MERCURY IS NUMBER ONE.
FIRST TO MEET THE HOT. HOT SUN.

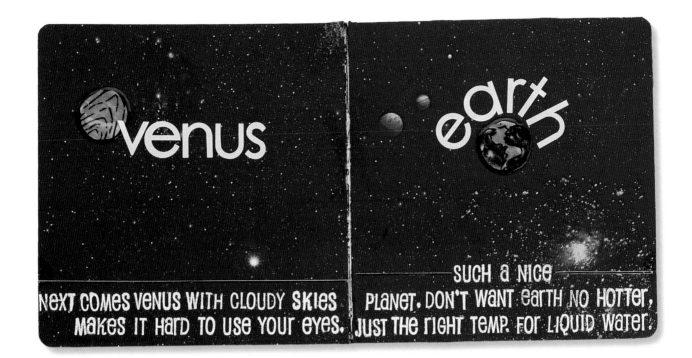

venus

NEXT COMES VENUS WITH CLOUDY SKIES
MAKES IT HARD TO USE YOUR EYES.

earth

SUCH A NICE
PLANET. DON'T WANT EARTH NO HOTTER,
JUST THE RIGHT TEMP. FOR LIQUID WATER.

STORY SUMMARIES

Once Upon a Time
by Julia Kruljac
On the island of Fairiopolis, deep in the enchanted forest, two little girls get lost at a fork in the road. They end up in Butterfly Village, where a butterfly points the way home.

The Little Girl
by Caitlin Joy Banks
A little girl is happiest playing with her family and friends, and drawing and writing poetry in school.

Magical and Me
by Hayley Peck
A peacock named Magical is lost in the woods and guided back home by a sweet little girl named Hayley.

Ode to the Planets
by Regan Jones
The reader is guided on a tour of the planets and their unique characteristics, through the poetic mind of a seven-year-old.

Going to See the Ring

On a vacation flight to New York City, to hear Richard Wagner's Ring Cycle operas performed on four consecutive nights, my inspiration occurred. I was reading the Siegfried chapter in M. Owen Lee's Wagner's Ring: Turning the Sky Round *where he recounts a version of Cinderella's tale that doesn't appear on film or in most books. I grabbed my little black book and hastily sketched a plan for my book (see page 13).*

ARTIST
Terry Taylor

Finished Dimensions
11¼ x 7½ inches (28.6 x 19 cm) (closed)
11¼ x 45 inches (28.6 x 114.3 cm) (open)

e brought her the
twig which she
ed on her mother's
grave and
watered it
with her
tears.

It grew
to become
a beautiful
tree.

Each time she did so
a pretty little bird would
come to her and tell her
what she needed to know.

the end

Materials and Tools

Watercolor paper

Vintage books

Photocopier

Blender pen

Matte acrylic varnish

Black silhouette paper

Spray adhesive

Rubber stamp alphabet

Ribbon

Hook-and-loop fasteners

Working Process

1. Envisioning an operatic theme, I pictured some of the imagery being drawn from a book I owned: *Physical Education in the Public Schools* (1892). I knew there were pictures of young women posing with "artistic expression" in the book. Eventually I decided to combine silhouette imagery—twig, tree, and bird—with solvent transfers of photocopied figures (see page 24).

2. I tore watercolor paper to size for the height of the pages. In order to create a length of paper for the accordion-fold book I had in mind, I joined two pieces of paper together, overlapping the paper at a point where the fold would hide the joint.

3. I used a photocopy machine to enlarge the figures to fit on the pages. With a blender pen and bone folder, I burnished the images onto the watercolor paper. To protect the images, I sprayed them with a light coat of matte acrylic varnish.

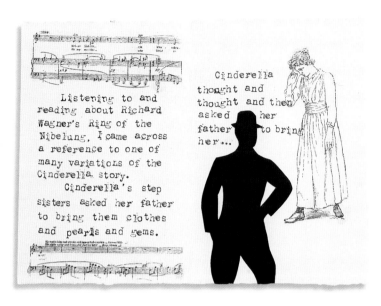

Listening to and reading about Richard Wagner's Ring of the Nibelung, I came across a reference to one of many variations of the Cinderella story.

Cinderella's step sisters asked her father to bring them clothes and pearls and gems.

Cinderella thought and thought and then asked her father to bring her...

"The first twig that touches your hat."

He brought her the leafy twig which she planted on her mother's grave and watered it with her tears.

It grew to become a beautiful tree.

Cinderella would visit the tree three times a day.

Each time she did so a pretty little bird would come to her and tell her what she needed to know.

the end

4. I found various patterns for birds and leafy twigs in different craft books. I adapted and reduced the size of the patterns before I photocopied them. I stapled the photocopies to black silhouette paper—strong, smooth paper used for paper cutting—and cut out the patterns with sharp scissors and a craft knife. I adhered the silhouettes to the pages using spray adhesive.

5. Text was added to the pages using rubber stamps in a typewriter font. I chose the font because the typewriter was a modern invention at the time that Wagner was composing the operas of the Ring Cycle.

6. I decided to recycle the cover from my copy of *The Victor Book of the Opera*—it was falling apart—to embellish the front of my storybook. I photocopied a male figure from the physical education book and sized it to fit the book cover. Then, I sketched a horned helmet on the figure, stapled the photocopy to silhouette paper, and cut it out. I affixed the figure to the cover with spray adhesive, and also made a smaller photocopy of the cover.

7. Rather than throw away the remains of the book, I reassembled the pages that described the four operas of the Ring Cycle. I carefully arranged the pages in matching pairs, glued a strip of rice paper to join each pair, and then bound the pages in a simple pamphlet. Inside the pamphlet, I added a glassine envelope that contains small photocopies of my Ring Cycle tickets. I added the small photocopy of the front cover to the pamphlet and embellished it with a photocopy of a vintage photograph of an opera star from the late part of the nineteenth century.

8. I cut four strips of black ribbon and glued them in a cross shape on the accordion book. I glued the book cover onto the accordion book and pressed it with heavy books overnight to prevent warping the paper. To finish, I added small hook-and-loop fasteners to the ends of the ribbons to secure the pamphlet to the larger book.

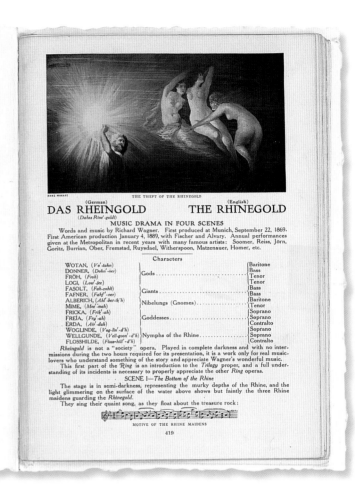

HANS MAKART   THE THEFT OF THE RHINEGOLD

(German)   (English)

DAS RHEINGOLD   THE RHINEGOLD
(Dahss Rine'-goldt)

MUSIC DRAMA IN FOUR SCENES

Words and music by Richard Wagner. First produced at Munich, September 22, 1869. First American production January 4, 1889, with Fischer and Alvary. Annual performances given at the Metropolitan in recent years with many famous artists: Soomer, Reiss, Jörn, Goritz, Burrian, Ober, Fremstad, Ruysdael, Witherspoon, Matzenauer, Homer, etc.

Characters

WOTAN, *(Vo'-tahn)*		Baritone
DONNER, *(Dohn'-ner)*	Gods	Bass
FRÖH, *(Froh)*		Tenor
LOGI, *(Low'-jee)*		Tenor
FASOLT, *(Fah-zohlt)*	Giants	Bass
FAFNER, *(Fahf'-ner)*		Bass
ALBERICH, *(Ahl'-ber-ik'h)*	Nibelungs (Gnomes)	Baritone
MIME, *(Mee'-meh)*		Tenor
FRICKA, *(Frik'-ah)*		Soprano
FREIA, *(Fry'-ah)*	Goddesses	Soprano
ERDA, *(Air'-dah)*		Contralto
WOGLINDE, *(Vog-lin'-d'h)*		Soprano
WELLGUNDE, *(Vell-goon'-d'h)*	Nymphs of the Rhine	Soprano
FLOSSHILDE, *(Floss-hill'-d'h)*		Contralto

Rheingold is not a "society" opera. Played in complete darkness and with no intermissions during the two hours required for its presentation, it is a work only for real music-lovers who understand something of the story and appreciate Wagner's wonderful music.

This first part of the *Ring* is an introduction to the *Trilogy* proper, and a full understanding of its incidents is necessary to properly appreciate the other *Ring* operas.

SCENE I—*The Bottom of the Rhine*

The stage is in semi-darkness, representing the murky depths of the Rhine, and the light glimmering on the surface of the water above shows but faintly the three Rhine maidens guarding the *Rhinegold*.

They sing their quaint song, as they float about the treasure rock:

MOTIVE OF THE RHINE MAIDENS

419

STORY INSPIRATION

In Siegfried—the third opera of the Ring Cycle—the hero searches for a mother who is unknown to him. In the opera, Siegfried wanders in a forest, singing "where is my mother?" He is soon answered by the trill of an unseen bird, bringing him some comfort. In Cinderella, the young orphan girl, besieged by evil stepsisters, longs for the care and guidance of her late mother. Like Siegfried, Cinderella draws comfort from the magical bird that appears in the tree she has planted. Both stories deal with the absence of the mother, a frequent theme in many classic fairy tales and myths.

The Birthday Gift

This delightful storybook combines artistry, collage, and a charming protagonist who overcomes the odds—and the forecast—to make the most of a dreadfully dry birthday.

the
birthday gift
by claudine hellmuth

ARTIST
Claudine Hellmuth

Finished Dimensions
10⅜ x 10⅜ inches (26.4 x 26.4 cm)

Working Process

1. Claudine's mother was the inspiration for this darling little storybook. When Claudine's mother was young, she received an umbrella as a birthday present, an oddly practical gift for a little girl but marvelous nonetheless. She was thrilled but had to wait six whole weeks before the next rain to use her treasured umbrella. Claudine's story follows a similar plot, with a slight twist at the end.

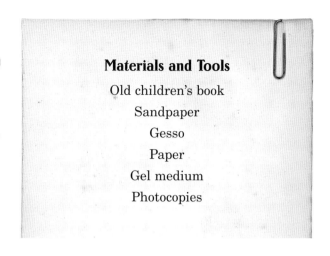

2. Now that she had her heroine and her story, Claudine set to work creating her book. First, she sanded down an old children's board book and then glued the pages together to make the right number she needed for her story.

3. Claudine painted the pages with gesso and allowed them to dry. With her "canvas" prepared, Claudine set about mapping each page. She made photocopies of the images she wanted to incorporate. Using these images and a little artistic inspiration, Claudine created collaged illustrations for each of her pages.

4. To add a bit of depth, Claudine drew in the ink lines. She typed lines of text on a computer. After cutting out the lines of text, Claudine added the text to each page to tell the story.

5. To create the cover, Claudine printed text on her computer, making sure to flip the text so that it was backwards. She applied gel medium to the cover and placed the printed text facedown in the wet gel. When the gel medium dried, she wet the back of the paper and removed it, leaving the text behind.

Materials and Tools
Old children's book
Sandpaper
Gesso
Paper
Gel medium
Photocopies

I waited
and waited
for rain so
I could
use my
new umbrella ...

STORY SUMMARY

A little girl receives an umbrella for her birthday. She is very excited and can't wait to use it. She waits and waits for rain to come, but each day is sunnier than the next. Finally, she decides to stop waiting for the rain and goes outside to play with her cherished umbrella, rain or no rain!

The Magpie & the Princess

LK gave her daughter the nickname Magpie even before her birth. For this book, LK wanted to create a story where a magpie is the hero rather than the harbinger of bad tidings or a thief, as is so often the case in stories from Western cultures. True to the proclivities of a magpie, this book is a veritable trove of tiny, shiny treasures.

ARTIST
LK Ludwig

Finished Dimensions
10 x 8 inches (25.4 x 20.3 cm)

Materials and Tools

Victorian photo album

Ribbons, tassels, decorative trim

Vintage ephemera

Antique photo frame

Decorative papers

Gel pen

Rubber stamps

Stencils or masking materials

Brass wire mesh

Rubber cement

Patina solution

Decorative brads and ribbon

Spray paints

Label maker

Brass lamp trim (a flexible
metal available online)

Fern fronds, fresh or silk

Repositionable spray adhesive

Beads, briolettes, and silver chain

Working Process

1. Working with vintage materials almost always requires a bit of ingenuity—papers can be brittle, bindings are loose, adhering dimensional items to other surfaces can be tricky. The binding on the cloth-covered Victorian photo album LK chose to use was less than pristine. In order to strengthen the binding, LK glued the last two pages to the back cover. She also removed pages to accommodate the thickness of the finished pages she envisioned. Rather than utilize the structure of the album's pages (see photo), LK envisioned covering each page entirely.

2. LK created a flow chart of the story (see page 12). She dedicated each spread to a scene in the story and tucked a sticky note on each page to remind her of what she intended to do on that particular page.

ONCE
UPON
A
TIME
A MAGPIE LIVED IN A FARAWAY FOREST

3. Many artists prefer to begin their books by creating the page spreads, but LK prefers to begin with the cover. An embroidered gold vine trim was glued to the cover first. Next LK created a collage for the title and framed it inside a vintage photo frame. She glued the frame to the cover using a heavy-duty glue.

4. Contemporary decorative papers echo the feeling that LK wanted her story to evoke. She covered each of the marked page spreads with one or more papers. A combination of china marker, gel pen, and alphabet rubber stamps were used to further enhance her vision for the finished composition.

5. LK used stencils and a fine mesh brass screen to create the "Once upon a time" page. Masks—simple letter forms—were secured to the mesh with rubber cement, which was also painted onto the screen as a mask for the cut-out shapes in the stencils.

LK applied a commercial patina solution to the brass mesh. When the desired color was achieved, LK rinsed the mesh with water and dried it thoroughly. The mesh was attached to the page with decorative brads. Ribbon was added to tie the following pages together.

6. The next page of LK's story was created using four different stencils to embellish a decorative sheet of paper. Once she was happy with the effect, she applied the magpie image. LK created a simple stencil for the branch. She drew the image onto cardstock and cut it out with a sharp craft knife. Several colors of paint were applied to create the mottled appearance of the branch. After the layers of paint were dry, the branch was outlined with gel pen. A label maker was employed to make the text. After the next page was completed, brass lamp trim and a tassel were added.

FRIENDSHIP BLOSSOMED

7. Ferns were used as masks on the brass mesh for the "her tears turned to jewels as they fell" page and were stenciled as described above. Spray adhesive was used to fix the ferns to the mesh during the patina process. If you're averse to picking live ferns (or you live in a desert climate), you can easily substitute silk fern fronds for fresh. LK added small briolettes and beads to the mesh with wire. Text was written onto small pieces of coordinating paper with a gel pen.

8. The "Friendship Blossomed" spread was stenciled using a vinyl place mat as a mask, a commercial stencil, and a hand-cut stencil. More briolettes and beads were wired to a bit of sterling chain. Small decorative blossoms were cut from a spray of artificial flowers. LK used a label maker to create the text. Brass lamp trim and tassels finished the page.

STORY SUMMARY

In the forest where the magpie lived, a princess was imprisoned in a castle. She sat each day in the window of her tower and cried out of loneliness, fear, and homesickness. As her tears fell from her tower perch, they turned to jewels. The magpie spied the jewels, as he is drawn to bright and beautiful shiny things, and began to collect them each day. An unlikely friendship blossomed, and the magpie was determined to help his friend. The magpie made a necklace from the jewels and took them to a prince in a neighboring kingdom. This brave prince rescued the princess, and they all lived happily ever after. The magpie was their lifelong friend.

Frau Trude

Jane chose the fable of Frau Trude for its simple message: "Do as your parents tell you, and nothing bad will happen to you." To add to the foreboding story, she created tension by using a childlike illustrative style within a grown-up construction showcasing a sparrow's leg wrapped in copper wire.

ARTIST
Jane Wynn

Finished Dimensions
5 x 4½ inches (12.7 x 11.4 cm)

People with...
One day she told her parents
I have heard so much of
Frau Trude, I will go to her some day.

Materials and Tools

18-gauge copper sheet

Silver solder

Vintage glass beads, brads,
and eyelets

Sparrow leg

24-gauge copper wire

Clear acrylic sheet

Thin, plastic cards

Cardstock

Vintage papers

Clear transparency sheet

Copper pipe

Plastic doll arm

Working Process

1. Jane started with the cover to determine the overall size of the book. With a jeweler's saw, she cut two copper squares and then drilled three holes in each for the binding. She heated the metal with the flame of a jeweler's torch to create a darker, uneven color, and allowed it to cool.

2. Jane then cut out four copper strips to form the sides of the little box on the cover. She soldered the four sides together to create a frame, then soldered the frame to the box.

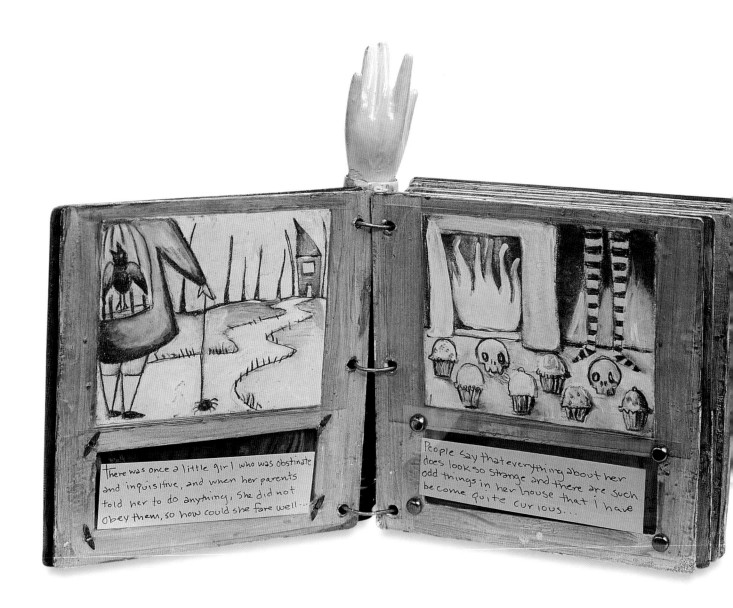

She created a background of vintage text in the box. For movement, Jane added a few silver glass seed beads and a sparrow's leg that she had partially wrapped with copper wire. To protect the materials in the box, Jane cut a clear acrylic sheet to size with a jeweler's saw and affixed it with two-part epoxy.

3. Using the size of the book cover as a guide, Jane created a paper template for the pages, cutting out areas for the small windows. She used the template to mark the shape onto thin, plastic cards. Jane glued recycled magazine pages—the heavier stock advertising is printed on—to the plastic cards. This created a

surface she could paint on easily. Jane then painted each covered page with acrylic paint to obscure the printed images.

4. Jane created the illustrations for the story on cardstock. She drew the images in pencil, adding thin washes of acrylic paint. She used white glue to affix the illustrations to the pages.

5. Using blank pages from a vintage book, Jane then wrote the text of the story with a fine black pen. She trimmed the text to fit inside the cutout window on each page.

Her parents absolutely forbade her and said FrauTrude is a bad woman who does wicked things and if you go to her you are no longer our child.

But the maiden did not let herself be turned aside by her parents prohibition, and still went To Frau Trude...

And when she got to her, Frau Trude said why are you so pale...

Ah, she replied and her whole body trembled, I have been so terrified at what I have seen. What have you seen?

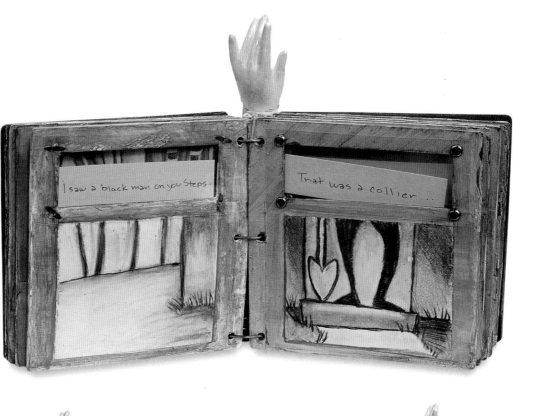

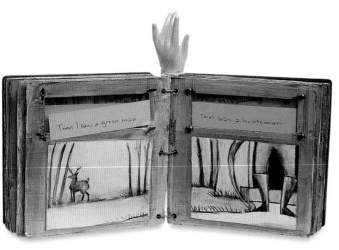

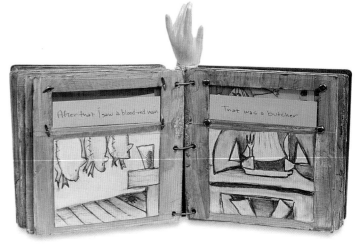

6. To secure the text, Jane cut out rectangles from a clear transparency sheet, making them slightly larger than each window. She punched holes in the corners of the window cutouts and then punched matching holes in the plastic rectangles. Jane secured the text between rectangles on both sides of the page, and fastened the rectangles with brads.

7. Using the covers as templates, Jane marked and punched holes in each page for the binding.

8. She cut a length of copper pipe to create a spine for the book and drilled three holes in the pipe, lining them up with the holes in the cover. Jane threaded copper wire through the pages and covers, and then threaded the wire through the pipe. Additional wire was wrapped around the pipe.

9. Jane adorned the top of the pipe with a plastic doll hand, which she painted, then sprayed with clear acrylic sealer.

STORY SUMMARY

In this little-known tale from the Brothers Grimm, a young girl's curiosity gets the best of her, when, despite her parents' warning, she seeks out the notoriously wicked Frau Trude. When the girl approaches Frau Trude's house, she has terrifying visions. She tells Frau Trude what she saw and is turned into a block of wood, which Frau Trude then throws into the fire for warmth and light.

Little Fatties

In this storybook the "ending" occurs in the middle. Identical sisters separately ponder different ideas, but discover, when their stories converge in the middle, that they think alike! Julie created her little fatties as American twin sisters that conjure good-hearted mischief and imperceptible charm.

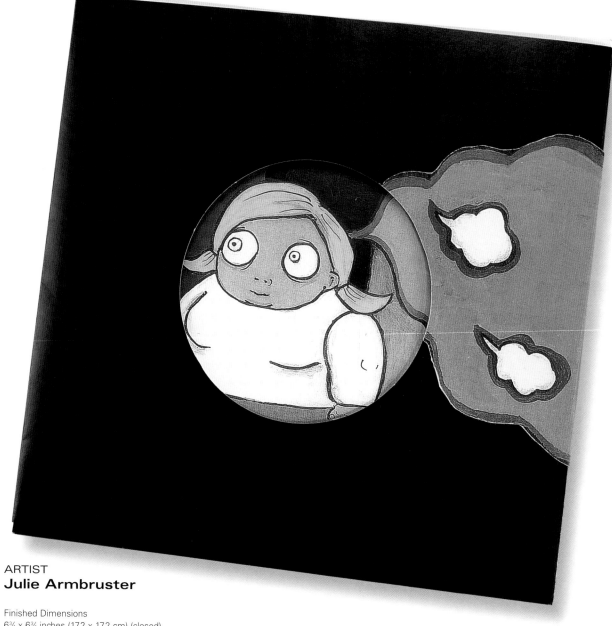

ARTIST
Julie Armbruster

Finished Dimensions
6¾ x 6¾ inches (17.2 x 17.2 cm) (closed)
6¾ x 42 inches (17.2 x 106.7 cm) (open)

Working Process

Materials and Tools

Pine panels (various sizes)

Gesso

Ink

Color photocopier

Black artists' tape

7-inch (17.8 cm) record jacket
with die-cut hole

1. Julie drew inspiration for her paintings from a news media story about the "xiao pangzi," or "little fatties," of China. These roly-poly children are the products of overindulgent parents, too much fast food, and not enough physical exercise. The individual panels are pine, primed with a homemade gesso—a mixture of water, white gesso pigment, flour, honey, linseed oil, and yellow ocher pigment based on traditional Italian recipes.

2. After priming several blocks with gesso, Julie started out by pushing ink around a primed wood block, giving the materials and the process a chance to reveal an image. The "little fatty" character had appeared in two earlier paintings, so when she started to peek out of the ink wash, Julie was able to form her easily. She used the same process on additional panels in the series, engaging the characters in wildly imaginative scenarios.

3. Julie arranged several panels in the series and set them side by side to begin constructing a narrative. The panels were of varying lengths and heights, but all of them were less than 14 inches (35.6 cm) in any dimension. Their size made it easy to visualize and structure the story. Later, the small size of the paintings made it easier to photocopy the images.

4. Once the story was conceived, Julie sketched each panel onto copy paper. She needed to unify the images and create a narrative. Julie thought of two more amusing scenarios in which the sisters could imagine themselves, and sketched them loosely on copy paper with a marker.

5. Since Julie's work is more visual than verbal, Julie created a playful title to accompany each of the frames that reflected the "imagination adventure." These titles then became the "text" of the story.

6. Julie visualized linking the paintings in an accordion-style book, so she taped the backs of the copy-paper versions together. The story begins with each sister on either end and ends in the center. At the center of the book, the girls high-five each other and are wearing the other sister's imagined costumes. It becomes clear that they are not just identical twins, but that they also share the same imagination.

7. Once all the paintings were completed and the story line in place, Julie photocopied each painting, reformatting their size and adding strips of black as needed. She added a single margin of black at the top of the panels.

Julie then created "thought bubbles" on which to letter the text. She settled on using a whimsical cursive for lettering. Once each element of text was finished, she affixed them to the photocopies.

8. Final photocopies were made of the pages, trimmed as needed, and then assembled with black artists' tape.

9. As a final touch, Julie created a customized 7-inch (17.8 cm) record jacket, with the little fatty faces peeking out of the die-cut center hole. She printed a final copy of the thought bubble from the first and last panel onto sticker paper, added them to the cover, and trimmed them as needed with a craft knife.

STORY SUMMARY

Chubby twin sisters dream up ideas for fun. Each sister imagines wild scenarios and eventually realizes that her identical twin already knew what she was thinking.

Old Hickory

Artist Susan McBride commissioned bookmaker Annie Fain Liden to create this richly textured book that folds out and can be displayed like a shrine. In it, Susan tells the story of a childhood summer spent in a cabin in the woods with beautiful, haunting illustrations featuring hand-cut stencils, stamps, paint, and collage.

ARTISTS
**Annie Fain Liden
& Susan McBride**

Finished Dimensions
8 x 12 inches (20.3 x 30.5 cm)

Book Materials

Two found book covers

Book board

Decorative paper

Lightweight text paper

Mixed papers

Irish waxed linen

Bookbinding glue

2 large buttons

Illustration Materials

Cardboard (for stencils)

Decoupage medium

Hand-carved stamps

Commercial stamps

Stamping ink

Collage materials

Working Process

1. Annie used covers from old books to create the front covers for this book. She cut covers off of two different books for the front, placed them side by side, and cut them into a somewhat asymmetrical house shape. She traced each shape to use as templates for the text pages.

2. She cut a single piece of book board for the back cover using the two front covers as a template. She covered the book board with decorative paper.

3. Annie used a mixture of paper types to create the pages. She created a total of eight signatures made up of six pages each—four signatures for each side of the book. She trimmed each stack of signatures to follow the "roof" line of each cover.

4. Annie used a used a multi-needle, Coptic-link stitch to bind the four signatures together. This binding is basically a series of crisscrossing and link stitches with subtle variations for adding the front and back covers. It is an exposed binding so the sewing is visible on the spines and is perfect for journaling or drawing because it lies flat when open.

5. Susan chose to paint different scenes using acrylic paint because it dries quickly, and she wanted to move through the book creating free and fluid illustrations.

My best friend lived on the same street.

Her name was Annie.

Annie and I were so excited about our trip.

When I was 7, I was invited up to her family's cabin

It took 2 hours to drive up to the cabin from the city.

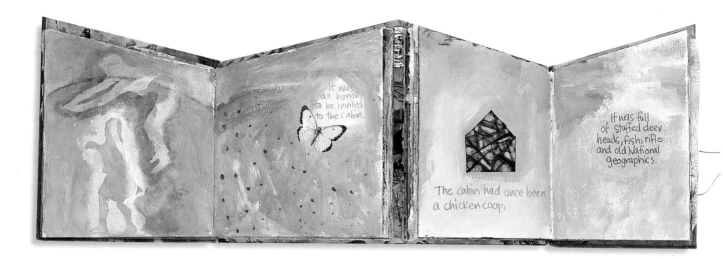

It was an honor to be invited to the cabin.

The cabin had once been a chicken coop.

It was full of stuffed deer heads, fish, rifles and old National geographics.

The cabin was in the woods. There was no indoor plumbing.

We didn't mind.

It was full of stuffed deer heads, fish, and old National geographic.

A river ran past the front of the cabin.

6. She used hand-cut stencils of children in active poses to animate the characters. The stencils were made from cardboard and then cut out with a craft knife. Susan pressed the stencils down on the paper, held them in place, and used a flat-edged brush with just a bit of acrylic paint. These silhouettes represent the ghosts of childhood and the memory of a different time.

At sunset one evening, the three of us were walking home from the gentleman's farm. We passed an apple tree on the way. Betse suddenly tore a limb from the tree, plucked a green apple and jammed it on to the pointed end of the stick. Then angrily whipped the apple into the mown field.

We joined her in this. It was cathartic to pull the fruit from the tree and sacrifice it to some inner force that felt like hidden rage.

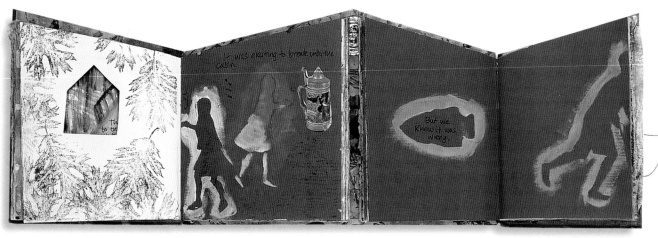

It was exciting to break into the cabin.

But we knew it was wrong.

7. To illustrate the industrial city of Susan's hometown, she used hand-carved stamps printed on mulberry paper, and adhered the pages to the book with decoupage medium.

8. As the story progresses into the mountains and to a river, Susan used more paint in large, flat surfaces to portray the landscape. She wanted to convey the free and open feeling experienced from leaving the oppressive cityscape and exploring the wilds of the mountain. The use of insect cutouts from a 1960s' guide was the perfect choice to interact with the stencils and stamps.

Suddenly, the three of us dropped our sticks and ran up the hill to the cabin. I have never been so afraid in my life.

We were completely spooked—but never discussed the incident.

STORY SUMMARY

A young girl is invited to join her best friend on a trip to the family cabin outside the city. Despite its rustic setting and lack of modern amenities, the cabin and its surroundings become a magical playground for the girls. The girls spend their days frolicking in the river, exploring neighboring houses, and picking fruit, learning much about themselves in the process.

The Mystery of the Royal Robe

Using bones, carved beads, and other relics, this storybook channels ancient mystery. Opie and Linda O'Brien worked in tandem to create this storybook in the hopes of providing the reader a glimpse into the mysterious world of the Aztec civilization, a continuous source of inspiration for their art.

ARTISTS
Opie and Linda O'Brien

Finished Dimensions
9 x 9½ inches (22.9 x 24.1 cm) (closed)
9 x 58 inches (22.9 x 147.3 cm) (open)

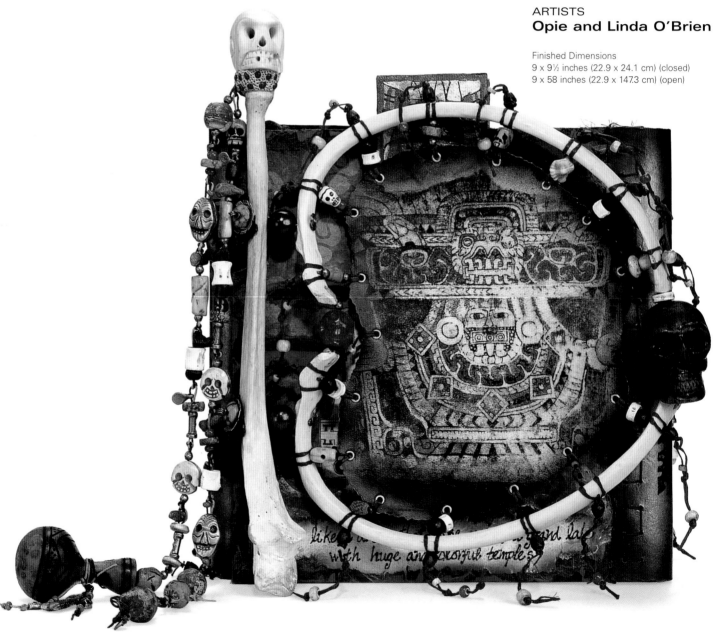

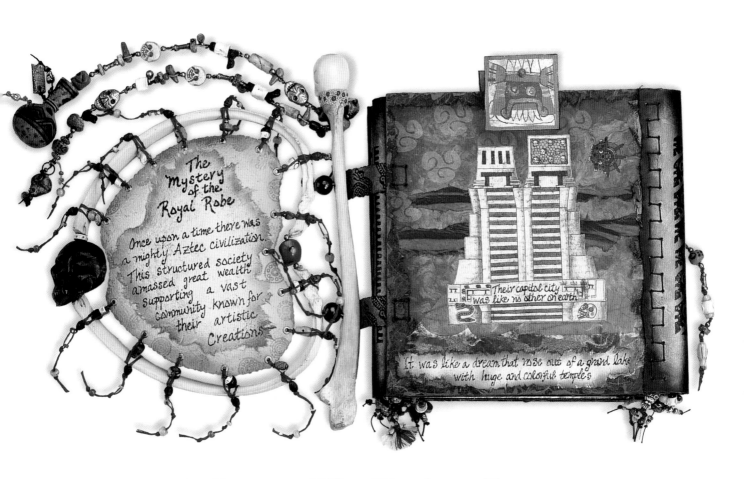

The Mystery of the Royal Robe

Once upon a time there was a mighty Aztec civilization. This structured society amassed great wealth supporting a vast community known for their artistic creations.

Their capital city was like no other on earth

It was like a dream that rose out of a grand lake with huge and colorful temples

Working Process

Materials and Tools

Bones and animal skin

Sinew and waxed linen

Various beads

Eyelets

Assorted wire and metals

Gourd

Wood putty or epoxy

Book board

Natural papers

PVA glue

Paint, ink, and dye

Gold and copper leaf

Fabric bits and fibers

Encaustic wax

Aztec imagery

Ink-jet canvas paper

1. Opie and Linda O'Brien have been going to Mexico since the mid-1980s and feel a strong connection to its history, its people, and its culture, so their choice for a storybook project seemed like a natural one. After carefully planning their storybook on a large sheet of newsprint, Opie constructed the frame for the book's cover by drilling holes in the ends of the curved bones (purchased in New York in 1994) and attaching beads with sinew.

2. Opie then transferred the image to the goat skin and punched holes around the perimeter of the skin, setting eyelets into each hole. Linda attached the skin to the bones with waxed linen and a variety of beads.

3. Opie attached the large skull bead to the top of the straight bone at the book's spine, wrapping strands of waxed linen underneath the skull bead and then covering the strands with a thin coat of wood putty in which he embedded tiny coral beads. To create the knotted waxed-linen dangles, Linda used a variety of shells, beads, artifacts, and a tiny wood-burned gourd.

4. Opie and Linda created the book's pages with book board, carefully cutting out the shapes at the top of each page. They sanded and sprayed each page with flat black paint. Once dry, they glued mulberry paper to the perimeter of each page, followed by a layer of bark paper with torn and feathered edges.

TIP: To keep the book board from warping as the glue dried, Linda and Opie used a book press with the pages sandwiched between freezer paper. If you don't have a book press, you can use heavy books to weigh down your pages.

5. To add highlights, Opie and Linda brushed encaustic wax (a colored painting medium) on the edges of each page. They covered the special cutouts at the top of each page with printed canvas images taken from ancient Codex books. They then used a wood-burning tool to inscribe the text on each page, adding additional embellishments with wire wrapping.

6. To fashion the book's spines, Linda and Opie cut four strips of cowhide. Then they painted the strips, touched up the edges with black marker, and rubber-stamped them. They punched small holes into each spine and used it as a template to drill the holes in the book board. Using waxed linen, Opie stitched the leather spines to the pages with a stitch he learned from book artist Doris Arndt.

Throughout the cape the origins of their pictograph writing system were revealed

to the Scribes

The Aztec culture thrived for centuries under the guidance of their Emperor, he who was ... any ill wind was approaching!

Ancient prophecies of doom were re-emerging and consulting priests through ritual offering confirmed this

Visiters from another land were false. They were not mythological figures returning... they were

Invaders

El Diablo

As the prophecy unfolded the Emperor was determined to preserve his cultures Art by invoking the powers of his Magic Robe.

On the appointed day in the Venus Cycle, he would place the Royal Cape in the center of the massive calender Stone, invoking the Earth Monster God.

At that precise moment, all the arrows on the Sacred Sun Stone would point to the exact location of their hidden treasures.

To this present day it has been said that the Royal Robe has been dutifully preserved by the chosen faithful. It is believed that it's location was hidden in many clues placed in several surviving Codex books

Some say it has been lost to Antiquity while others say it is just a myth

The Search Continues

7. Linda and Opie created the hinges using two thin strips of the same cowhide, and finished them following the same steps used to create the spine. They attached the hinges by punching one hole at each end and passing a wire through the hinge and both bones, with a variety of beads interspersed for decoration.

STORY SUMMARY

This story tells the tale of the mighty Aztec civilization and their powerful emperor. The emperor was the owner of a magical robe that was decorated with fine jewels and shimmering metals and was, legend has it, once worn by the gods themselves. In addition to its beautiful adornments, the robe also held the origins of the Aztec writing system. Under the rule of the emperor, and his magic robe, the Aztec civilization flourished for many years, but ancient prophecies of doom re-emerged and invaders soon arrived. The emperor was determined to preserve his culture's art by invoking the powers of his magic robe, which would, if used properly, reveal the location of a vast treasure. What became of the robe is a mystery. Perhaps it has been lost to antiquity or maybe its existence is just a myth. However, the search continues.

Trussard and the Magic Seeds

With old sheet music, colorful cutouts, and vintage imagery, Sandra Evertson fashions a tale of hard work and magical harvest loosely based on Joseph Campbell's hero theme.

ARTIST
Sandra Evertson

Finished Dimensions
12½ x 7½ inches (31.1 x 19 cm)

Working Process

1. Collage is one of Sandra's favorite working techniques. Because she wanted to use collaged images in her ledger, she glued together several pages of the ledger before adhering images to the page (see page 16).

2. Sandra began assembling her book by creating backgrounds for her images. She glued vintage sheet music to her book pages to create the "ground," and collaged a variety of decorative papers to create the "sky." She created clouds by tearing out cloud shapes and shaded the edges with colored chalks. Decoupage medium was used to adhere the backgrounds to the ledger pages.

Materials and Tools

Vintage ledger journal

Vintage images

Sheet music

Vintage text

Decorative papers

Colored chalks

Oil pastels

Cardstock

3. Sandra creatively utilized a photocopier to create most of the images in her storybook. The sun image was originally a small black-and-white image that she enlarged, colored with chalks, and then photocopied to the size she needed. Using oil pastels, Sandra drew ovals, then reduced the images until they looked like the magic seeds. To create the little blooming creatures, Sandra made several copies of the images. For visual interest, many of the images were photocopied using the mirror image function. The pink and blue skunks began life as squirrels: Sandra photocopied the images in black and white, and then colored them.

Once all of the images were photocopied, colored, enlarged, reduced, and mirrored, Sandra affixed them to the background using decoupage medium.

and then CRASH, knocking him off his feet. Trussard looked up to find a very dapper donkey dressed in a very fine suit gently dusting himself off, and up turned wooden cart and many seed sacks scattered about.

"My name is Drewkell" said the donkey, "Ever so sorry, forgive the mishap, kind lad" as he gathered up his cache and strolled along his way.

Trussard in a bit of a huff noticed a stray sack of seeds and decided he would keep them for his troubles.

Now, a curious sort of seeds these were, like none he'd ever seen.

He raked and hoed and plowed his field, and ever so gently tucked one after the other in narrow little rows. And every single day when the sun came up Trussard would water and preen and chase away bugs,

till finally, tiny little yellow green tendrils began curling their way skyward. And with every passing day grew larger, and stronger, and greener. All the while Trussard could hardly wait to see what wondrous glorious kinds of things would bloom from those odd sorted seeds. The days turned into weeks, rains came, winds blew, Oh, when will those plants bloom!

And just as Trussard was beginning to lose hope, he heard a faint song coming from the garden. And running as fast as his feet could carry him, Lo, to his amazement, what did he see?

He rubbed his eyes twice and wiggled a finger in one ear. A fuzzy Pussy Willow bloomed with stripey yellow kittens. Short stocky hedges laden with speckled pups! And what else but Snap Dragons with,

4. Sandra cleverly created the text for her story using the "ransom note" technique. She cut out a wide variety of colorful and interesting letter fonts from magazines, books, greeting cards, and other printed texts. She created an alphabet and made several photocopies to cut apart to compose her text.

5. To create a vintage feel for the text, Sandra photocopied her assembled text onto tan card-stock. She adhered the text to the pages using decoupage medium.

STORY SUMMARY

A young boy named Trussard plants an odd packet of seeds that he receives from Drewkell, the donkey. After carefully tending to his seedlings, Trussard is rewarded with a mysterious crop of flowers that come to life in a magical way.

FEATURED ARTISTS

Julie Armbruster is a mixed-media painter who has studied traditional painting techniques in Venice, Italy. She integrates her social observations with an intu-

itive process and brings new life to the practice of figurative painting. Julie currently resides in West Asheville, North Carolina, with her husband and their pets, Weirdo, Spankie, and SwizzNoodle. See more of Julie's work at www.JulieArmbruster.net or www.myspace.com/juliearmbruster.

Amy Blandford began her art career early in life, winning her first major award for a safety awareness

poster. After receiving a BFA in Graphic Communications from the College for Creative Studies in Detroit, she worked for a time as a professional illustrator and now focuses on product development and packaging design for the giftware and home décor industry. Amy currently lives in southern California with her husband Ed.

Lisa Cook's love for vintage ephemera, found objects, and old textbooks was influenced by childhood trips to

antique stores with her grandmother and mother. Besides teaching a number of classes, Lisa and her designs have been in mixed-media books by Stampington & Company,

Lark Books, and Chapelle Ltd., as well as several magazines. Visit her online at www.lisacookstudio.com and www.opengate.typepad.com.

Sandra Evertson is a self-taught artist and a magpie collector of things old and unique, surrounding her

work space with things that inspire her to create. Sandra is the author of *Fanciful Paper Flowers* (Lark/Chapelle, 2007) and *Fanciful Paper Projects* (Sterling/Chapelle, 2005). She also serves as a Director's Circle Artist for Somerset Studio magazine. See more of her work at www.sandraevertson.blogspot.com.

Annie Fain Liden grew up near the John C. Campbell Folk School near Murphy, North Carolina, surrounded

by a community of professional craftspeople and musicians. She has studied book arts and paper-making at Penland School of Crafts. Annie lives and works in Asheville, North Carolina. Visit her website at www.afainbooks.com.

Terry Garrett is a native of southeastern Iowa and has a background in Art Education. Specializing in collage using his own photographic images, his work has appeared in three books and several magazines, as well as a

number of private collections. Terry now serves as an assistant professor in the visual arts department at Bemidji State University in Bemidji, Minnesota.

Erikia Ghumm is a mixed-media scrapbook artist, author, and instructor. Her work has been widely published in craft magazines and books, and she has

authored/co-authored two books. In addition, she is a contributing editor for *Better Homes and Gardens Scrapbooks etc.* See more of her projects online at www.erikiaghumm.com.

Lisa Glicksman is a mixed-media artist with a particular fondness for paper arts, rubber stamping, and painting. She looks for ways to incorporate her various collections into her work: vintage books and

toys, game pieces, and paper ephemera. Her work is exhibited locally and recently appeared in *Artful Paper Dolls* (Lark Books, 2006). Lisa lives in Oakland, California, with her husband Dan. Visit her online at www.glixart.com.

Claudine Hellmuth is the author of *Collage Discovery Workshop* and *Collage Discovery Workshop: Beyond the Unexpected* (North Light Books). She lives in

Orlando, Florida, and teaches workshops around the world. Visit her website at www.collageartist.com.

Margert Kruljac has been creating from the moment she touched her first crayon. She is a self-taught artist comfortable in all mediums and warns that no object is safe from her "altering ways." Margert

teaches at industry trade shows, as well as several times a month at her local scrapbook store. She also designs for two publications, and her work has

been featured in many others. She calls southern West Virginia home.

LK Ludwig is both an artist and author, living and working in her studio, The Gryphon's Feather Studio, in western Pennsylvania. Also a part-time instructor, LK's work can be found in a number of publications including several from Lark Books: *The Altered Object* (2006), *Artful Paper Dolls* (2006), and *Designer Needle Felting* (2007). She also has two forthcoming books (*Mixed Media Nature Journaling* and *True Vision: Authentic Art Journaling*) due out in 2008. Find out more at her website: gryphonsfeather.typepad.com.

Sharon Mann infuses her love for traditional needle-craft with other craft techniques, producing imaginative projects that are both dimensional  and novel. Featured in several magazines and online, her recent published work includes *Kooky Crochet* (Lark Books, 2007) and *Crochet Kid Stuff* (Creative Publishing international and Coats and Clark Crochet and Knitting booklets, 2007). Visit her website at www.sharonmanndesigns.com.

Susan McBride is an artist who has worked in the field of graphic design for the last 20 years. She has sketched and painted all of her life. She's the author  and illustrator of *The Don't-Get-Caught Doodle Notebook* (Lark Books, 2005), *The I'm-So-Bored-Doodle Notebook* (Lark Books, 2006), and *Office Doodle Notebook* (Lark Books, 2007). She lives in Asheville, North Carolina, with her family, two cats, and a crazy dog.

Catherine Moore is a mixed-media artist and illustrator residing in Peachtree City, Georgia. Her work has  been published in contemporary books and magazines, and her illustrations are the creative impetus behind a collection of rubber stamps for creating paper dolls. Catherine teaches a variety of workshops throughout the country. You can see more of her work at www.CharacterConstructions.com.

Opie and **Linda O'Brien** are mixed-media artists, authors, and teachers who consider themselves "caretakers of the mundane and the ordinary." Their projects have been featured in over 20 books, in sev-  eral magazines, and in numerous art galleries. New York transplants, they now live in Ohio on Lake Erie with their cat Angelus and his cat Angel. For more information, visit their website at www.burntofferings.com.

Jane Reeves's work has been widely exhibited and is included in numerous publications. Her favorite art materials are cheesecloth, rusty nails, and vintage  magazines. Jane lives and works in Black Mountain, North Carolina, where she enjoys using fabric, paper, and found objects to make art quilts, collages, and mixed-media constructions.

Karen Shelton was born in San Francisco, California, and has been making her own storybooks since age five. While her dad helped her make the first few using construction paper and crayons, Karen now has a very large collection of altered books and journals. She lives in Pepperell, Massachusetts, and is very active in the 1001 Journals Project.

Andrea Stern started her artistic pursuits with simple drawings and soon progressed to painting, beadwork, and quilting. Supported by a family of artists, Andrea received a formal degree in art history in 1990, but it  wasn't until owning her own bead business that she really learned to apply the principles of design she learned in school. Examples of her work are available at www.embellishmentcafe.com or andibeads.blogspot.com.

Terry Taylor is an acquisitions editor at Lark Books. He's the author of several books including *Altered Art*  (Lark Books, 2004), *Artful Paper Dolls* (Lark Books, 2006), and *The Altered Object* (Lark Books, 2006). He's a jeweler in his spare time and prefers to spend his vacation time taking metalworking classes. His other passion requires him to fly around the country to see well-known opera companies perform.

Linda Trenholm is a member of Somerset Studio Director's Circle Artists. Working part-time as a Visual  Merchandising Coordinator with Tiffany & Co. affords her the opportunity to pursue her art, both in her studio and as a workshop instructor. Linda lives in Las Vegas with her husband Tom. View more of her work at www.latrenholm.com.

Jane Wynn grew up making art  as her focus and passion. After graduating with a BFA from the University of Maryland Baltimore County and an MFA from Towson University, Jane began teaching art at Towson University and the Community Colleges of Baltimore County. She lives in Baltimore, Maryland, with her husband, their four cats, some fish, and a very sassy scooter that they like to take for quick trips to local coffee spots. See more of Jane's work at www.wynnstudio.com.

Index